LADDERS to SUCCESS

on the New York State Test

English Language Arts

LEVEL **C**

LEVELED INSTRUCTION AND PRACTICE ON 10 ESSENTIAL SKILLS

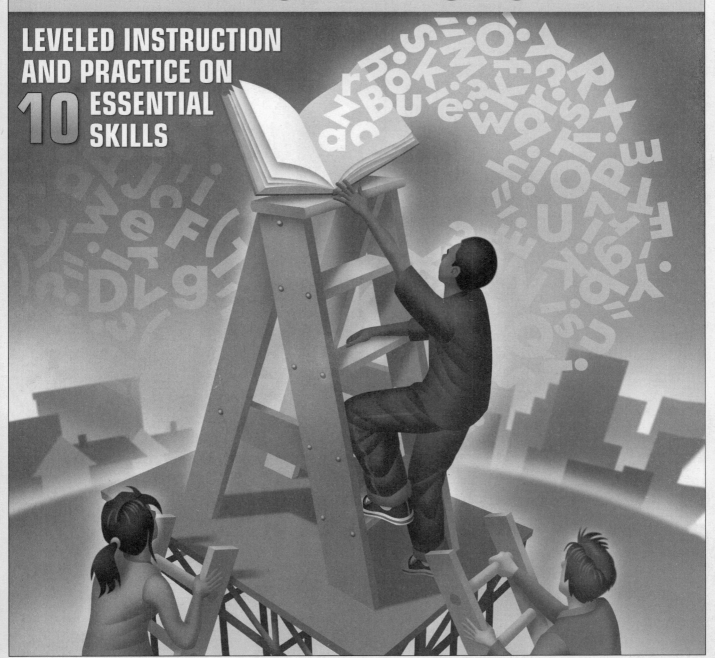

ACKNOWLEDGMENTS

"Students Make Their Own Menu" contains quotations courtesy of www.potomacnews.com

"Light Bulb Burns for 100 Years" contains quotations courtesy of Reuters

"Street Corners" by Susan A. DeStefano, copyright © 2006. Reprinted with permission of the author.

"Lion Cub and Puppy Become Friends" contains quotations courtesy of www.nctimes.com

"Ringling Brothers Circus Makes Big Changes" contains quotations courtesy of www.nytimes.com

Page 34-Punxsutawney Phil, Chris Hondros/Getty Images

Page 41-Boy on Bike, Justine Pumfrey/Getty Images

Page 48-Lopez brothers, Matthew Stockman/Getty Images

Page 49-Molasses spill, Corbis

Page 55-Hot-air Balloon, NASA

Page 76-Darth Vader, James Keyser/Getty Images

Page 90-Lightbulb, Jim Krantz/Getty Images

Page 111-Canstruction, Kathy Willens/Associated Press

Page 118-Two-headed Snake, World Aquarium/Corbis

Page 132-Elephants in Parade, Brendan Smialowski/Getty Images

Ladders to Success on the New York State Test, English Language Arts Level C
129NY
ISBN# 1-59823-471-4

EVP, Publisher: Bill Scroggie
VP, Editorial Director: Marie Spano
VP of Production: Dina Goren
Art Director: Farzana Razak

Senior Development Editor: Elizabeth Jaffe
Editorial Development: Chrysalis Publishing Group
Designer: Farzana Razak
Cover Design: Farzana Razak
Cover Illustration: Sam Ward/Mendola Artists

Triumph Learning® 136 Madison Avenue, New York, NY 10016-6711
© 2007 Triumph Learning, LLC

A Haights Cross Communications, Inc. company

Printed in the United States of America.

10 9 8 7 6 5 4 3 2 1

Table of Contents

New York State Standards

Letter to the Student

Dear Student,

Welcome to **Ladders to Success** for Level C. This book will help you work on the ten reading skills most important to you this year. There is one lesson for each skill. You will master all ten skills by working through all ten lessons one by one.

This book does not rush you through a skill. Each lesson is fourteen pages long. This gives you plenty of time to really get comfortable learning what each skill means. You will see how each skill works in stories of different lengths.

The first page of every lesson is called Show What You Know. Take this short quiz to see how much you know about a skill before digging into the lesson. The next section, Guided Instruction 1, will start you off with some friendly guided review and practice. Practice the Skill 1, which follows Guided Instruction 1, shows you how to answer a multiple-choice question before asking you to try more by yourself. The next section, News Flash, is an exciting news story. It also comes with an activity.

Following the first News Flash is a three-page section called Ladder to Success. This section will give you three chances to practice the skill. Each practice is a little harder as you go "up the ladder." Now you are ready for the second part of the lesson.

The second part of the lesson is just like the first. You will see Guided Instruction 2, Practice the Skill 2, and another News Flash. This time around, these sections are a little harder. The last two pages of each lesson are called Show What You Learned. Show off everything you learned in the lesson by correctly answering multiple-choice questions on the skill. Words that are boldfaced in the lessons appear in the glossary at the back of the book.

The lessons in this book will help you practice and improve your skills. They will also get you ready for the tests you will be taking this year. Some of the practice will be in the style of the state test. You will be answering multiple-choice and open-ended questions. You may see questions like these on your state test. Practicing with these types of questions will build your confidence.

We hope you will enjoy using *Ladders to Success.* We want you to climb the ladder to success this year. This book will help you get started!

Letter to the Family

Dear Parent or Family Member,

The **Ladders to Success** series of workbooks is designed to prepare your child to master ten of the fundamental skills in reading that are essential for success, both in the curriculum and on state tests. *Ladders to Success* provides guided review and practice for the skills that are the building blocks of your child's education in reading. These are also the skills that will be tested on the state test in English/Language Arts. Your child's success will be measured by how well he or she masters these skills.

Ladders to Success is a unique program in that each lesson is organized to ensure your child's success. Ten skills that students often find challenging are treated individually in ten lessons. Students are guided and supported through the first part of each lesson until they are ready to take on unguided practice in the second part of the lesson. Each lesson is fourteen pages long to give the student ample opportunity to review and practice a skill until a comfort level is reached. Support is gradually withdrawn throughout the lesson to build your student's confidence for independent work at the end of each lesson.

We invite you to be our partner in making learning a priority in your child's life. To help ensure success, we suggest that you review the lessons in this book with your child. You will see how each lesson gets subtly but progressively harder as you go along. While teachers will guide your child through the book in class, your support at home, added to the support of guided instruction and practice in the series, is vital to your child's comprehension.

We ask you to work with us this year to help your young student climb the ladder to success. Together, we can make a difference!

Letter to the Teacher

Dear Teacher,

Welcome to **Ladders to Success** on the New York State Test in English Language Arts for Level C. The Ladders to Success series of workbooks for reading is designed to prepare your students to master ten fundamental, grade-appropriate skills in reading that are essential for success both in the curriculum and on your state tests. Ladders provides guided review and practice for the skills that are the building blocks of the students' education. These are also skills that will be tested on your state tests in reading.

Ladders to Success is a unique program in that each lesson is leveled, or scaffolded, to ensure your students' success. Students are guided and supported through the first part of each lesson until they are ready to take on unguided practice in the second part of the lesson. Ten important skills are treated individually in ten lessons. Each lesson is fourteen pages long to give the student ample opportunity to review and practice a skill until a comfort level is reached. Support is slowly withdrawn throughout the lesson to build your students' confidence for independent work at the end of each lesson.

Ladders has a consistent, symmetrical format. The format is predictable from lesson to lesson, which increases students' comfort level with the presentation of skills-based information and practice. The first page of every lesson is called Show What You Know. This is a short diagnostic quiz to determine how much a student knows about a particular skill before digging into the lesson. It represents a snapshot of where each student is "now" before additional review and practice. This diagnostic quiz can be your guide in the way you choose to use the different parts of the lesson that follows.

The next section, Guided Instruction 1, will start students off slowly with guided review and practice. Practice the Skill 1, which immediately follows Guided Instruction 1, models how to answer a multiple-choice question before asking students to try more by themselves. The next section, News Flash, is an exciting contemporary news story that will engage students' interest. It is accompanied by an activity, often a graphic organizer, under the heading Write About It.

Following the first News Flash is a three-page section called Ladder to Success, which embodies the spirit of the Ladders series. This section provides three more chances to practice the skill. What makes this section unique is that each practice is a little harder as students go "up the ladder." By the time students have finished the third practice, they are ready for the second part of the lesson, which mirrors the first part. The Ladder to Success section is the crucial bridge between the first part of the lesson and the second.

Thus, you will now see Guided Instruction 2, Practice the Skill 2, and another News Flash. This time around, however, these sections are more challenging. The passages are longer and/or cognitively more difficult and there is less modeling. The activity under the Write About It heading in the second News Flash in each lesson, for example, is an unscaffolded writing activity.

The last two pages of each lesson represent a Posttest on the skill of the lesson. It is called Show What You Learned. Here is the student's chance to show off everything he or she learned in the lesson by successfully answering multiple-choice questions on the skill. The Posttest ends with an open-ended question, giving students the opportunity to show a deeper understanding of the skill now that they have completed the lesson. Words that are bold-faced in the lessons appear in the glossary at the back of the book.

Triumph Learning supports you in the difficult challenges you face in engaging your students in the learning process. *Ladders to Success* attempts to address some of these challenges by providing lessons that contain interesting material; scaffolded, or leveled, support; and a spectrum of multiple-choice questions and open-ended activities. This will allow students to build their confidence as they work toward proficiency with each skill in each lesson.

We ask you to work with us this year to help your students climb the ladder to success. Together, we *will* make a difference!

LADDERS to SUCCESS

LESSON
1
Comparing and
Contrasting

Show What You Know

R3.3   Compare and contrast characters, plot, and setting in literary works, with assistance.

Before you begin this lesson, take this quiz. Show what you know about comparing and contrasting. Read this story about a girl's new room. Then answer the questions.

Annie's New Room

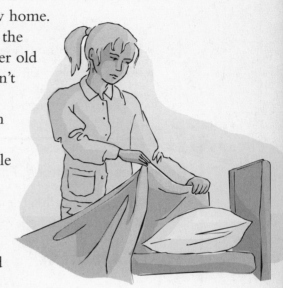

Annie looked around her new room in her family's new home. It didn't look exactly like her old room, but some of it was the same. For one thing, the walls were painted green, like in her old room. Her mom had wanted to paint them blue. Annie didn't want a new bedspread either. So her mom had washed the old blue striped quilt and put it back on her bed. The green walls and old quilt made Annie feel more at home.

The new room did have more space. Annie was now able to hang her extra posters on the walls. She also had a new desk. It was between the two large windows on the long wall. Annie's old room had one small window that looked out over trash cans in the back alley. From her new room, Annie could watch cars and people on the street. She could even see a park where kids her age were playing kickball.

Circle the letter of the best answer.

1. How are the walls in Annie's new room like the walls in her old room?

   A They are the same color.
   B They have space for extra posters.
   C They have large windows.
   D They need to be painted.

2. Which of these is the same in Annie's new room as it was in her old room?

   A The extra posters
   B The desk
   C The quilt
   D The windows

3. Which of these tells one way that Annie's new room is different from her old room?

   A The new room is square.
   B The new room is bigger.
   C The new room is painted green.
   D The new room is empty.

4. From her old room Annie could not see —

   A trash cans
   B anything
   C the alley
   D a park

LESSON

1

Comparing and
Contrasting

Guided Instruction 1

R3.3   Compare and contrast characters, plot, and setting in literary works, with assistance.

When you **compare,** you tell how things are alike. When you **contrast,** you tell how things are different.

To compare and contrast,

- First think about what is being compared or contrasted.
- Find comparison or contrast word clues, such as *alike* and *unlike.*
- Find details that tell how the people, places, things, or events are alike and different.

Here's How

Read these sentences. Find ways to compare and contrast the characters.

Like most of his friends, Vic joined the baseball team. Unlike his friends, who loved playing baseball, Vic did not enjoy it at all.

Think About It

1. I see that Vic and his friends are compared and contrasted.

2. The clue words *like* and *unlike* are used to compare and contrast.

3. I use the details to compare and contrast Vic and his friends. Vic is like his friends because he joined the baseball team. Vic is different from his friends because he doesn't enjoy playing baseball, but they love it.

Try This Strategy

Use Prior Knowledge

When you **use prior knowledge,** you think about what you know to understand what you read.

- Think about what you know about the subjects of the passage.
- Think about ways the characters in a story are like people you know.
- Use what you know about people, places, and things. This helps to understand what you read about a story's subject, characters, and so on.

Read the story. Use the Reading Guide for tips. The tips will help you use prior knowledge and compare and contrast as you read.

 Reading Guide

Look for a clue word that tells you the author is about to compare Vic to his friends.

Now look for clue words that point to differences between Vic and his friends.

Think about ways that kids try to be like their friends. Then think about how kids feel when they realize they are diferent. Use what you know to understand how Vic feels.

Think about how Vic felt when he played baseball. Then notice how karate made him feel.

A NEW SPORT FOR VIC

Like most of his friends, Vic joined the baseball team. Unlike his friends who loved playing baseball, Vic didn't enjoy it at all.

Vic's friends knew what to do on the field. They knew when to run and when to stay on base. They were able to throw the ball well. They had natural talent.

Vic, on the other hand, got mixed up easily. He threw the ball to the wrong place. He could hit okay, but he had no idea where or when to run. The coach was kind. His teammates were, too. But Victor felt bad when he made mistakes. He left the team.

Then Vic's mother signed him up for karate lessons. Vic's instructor said Vic had natural talent. Playing baseball had made Vic feel weak and unhappy. Karate was different. It made Vic feel strong and happy.

Vic still likes watching baseball, but karate is the sport for him.

Now use what you learned to compare and contrast.

Answer the questions on the next page.

Practice the Skill 1

R3.3   Compare and contrast characters, plot, and setting in literary works, with assistance.

Practice comparing and contrasting details in the story you just read.

EXAMPLE

What made Vic different from his friends when they were playing baseball?

A Vic got confused, but his friends knew what to do.

B Vic was a strong player, but his friends were weak.

C Vic had natural talent, but his friends didn't.

D Vic was happy, but his friends were unhappy.

Note what is compared and contrasted.

The author is contrasting Vic and his friends.

Look for clue words that signal comparisons and contrasts.

I see the clue words *on the other hand*. This tells me the author is about to make a contrast.

Find details that tell how characters are alike or different.

Vic's friends knew what to do on the field. Vic got mixed up easily. These details tell about the characters.

Now read each question. Circle the letter of the best answer.

1. How were Vic's coach and teammates alike?

    A They made Vic feel bad.

    B They were kind to Vic.

    C They sometimes made mistakes.

    D They wanted Vic to leave.

2. Which of these was hard for Vic, but not for his teammates?

    A Doing karate

    B Making friends

    C Hitting the ball

    D Throwing the ball

3. Karate was different for Vic because —

    A it made him happy

    B he didn't have to be strong

    C the instructor was kind

    D he didn't have to practice

4. Vic and his friends both —

    A knew when to run and stop

    B had natural talent

    C enjoyed just watching baseball

    D were unhappy

A family in Alaska built a 16-foot snowman.

Here Comes SNOWZILLA!

ANCHORAGE, AK—Can you imagine building a snowman taller than your house? Billy Ray Powers and his children did just that.

It started like other snowmen. The Powers **gathered** the snow in their yard. They made three round balls. Each one was a different size. They packed the snow firmly so that it would stay together.

Unlike other snowmen, this one grew bigger and bigger. After they used all the snow in their yard, they took snow from neighbors' yards. Soon, other children and friends started to help. The snowman grew so large that they had to use bottles for eyes. The arms were put in with a drill.

It took one month to finish the snowman. People have named it "Snowzilla." It is 16 feet tall. Visitors from all over the world have come to see it.

Write About It

Compare and contrast to fill in the chart below. On the left side, write facts that are only true about "Snowzilla." On the right side, write facts that are only true about regular-sized snowmen. At the bottom, write facts that are true about both.

Snowzilla	Snowman
Both	

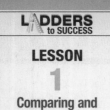

LESSON

1

Comparing and
Contrasting

Ladder to Success

R3.3   Compare and contrast characters, plot, and setting in literary works, with assistance.

Review

You have learned how to **compare and contrast** so that you can better understand what you read. As you read, look for ways people, places, things, and events are alike or different.

Review the steps you can use to compare and contrast.

- Think about what is being compared or what is being contrasted.
- Look for clue words that signal a comparison or contrast.
- Use story details to tell how people, places, things, or events are alike or different.

Practice 1

Read the following story. As you read, think about what the writer tells you about New York and Florida. Then look for details that tell how New York and Florida are alike and different for Rose.

> Rose moved from New York to Florida. When Rose left New York, the weather was freezing. She had worn her coat, hat, and gloves to the airport. In Florida, it was warm enough for Rose to wear shorts. Not everything had changed though. Rose still had to go to school and do chores. But instead of shoveling snow, she was weeding the garden.

Using the Venn diagram below, choose details from the story to show how Rose's life is different in Florida than it was in New York, and how it is the same.

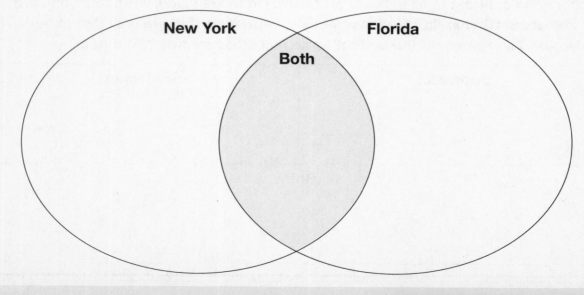

Practice 2

Read the passage. How are the two girls alike and different?

"I'm tired of being mistaken for Rena just because we both have brown hair and green eyes," Trina said.

"People should be able to tell twins apart," Rena said.

"You're right," Dad said. "But, you do look very much alike."

"Yes, but my hair is short while Rena's is long," Trina said.

"You both have big friendly smiles," Mom said.

"Well then maybe I should be a grump," Rena joked.

"My front teeth are a little crooked," Trina said. "Rena's are perfectly straight."

"That reminds me," Mom said. "The dentist called to **schedule** your checkups."

Trina frowned. "I have an idea. Since Dr. Lewis can't tell us apart either, Rena can go twice."

Use this graphic organizer to compare and contrast Rena and Trina.

Rena	Trina

Both

Practice 3

Read the passage. Then compare and contrast to answer the questions. Make a graphic organizer on a separate sheet of paper to organize your thoughts.

My brother Mike ran two races this summer. Both races were four miles long and both were held on holidays. The first race was in the middle of the summer. It was part of the town's Fourth of July picnic. The second race was on Labor Day, at the end of the summer. Mike trained hard for both races.

The Fourth of July was a steamy, hot day. Mike began at a slow pace. After a mile, he picked up speed and passed all the other runners. He was in first place when the heat finally got to him and he had to stop running. I don't think I've ever seen him so disappointed.

Unlike the Fourth of July, Labor Day was cool and cloudy. Mike began the race the same way as he had before, at a slow pace. Then he picked up speed. But this race was different from the first one. This time, Mike stayed in first place until he crossed the finish line. I've never seen Mike so happy.

1. How long were both races and when were they held?

   _____

   _____

2. What made the weather for the second race better than it was for the first race?

   _____

   _____

3. Compare and contrast how Mike ran and felt after each race.

   _____

   _____

LADDERS to SUCCESS

LESSON

1

Comparing and Contrasting

Guided Instruction 2

R3.3   Compare and contrast characters, plot, and setting in literary works, with assistance.

Writers **compare and contrast** to help you understand how people, places, things, and events are alike and different.

As you saw on pages 13–15, graphic organizers can help you compare and contrast.

- In the left circle, write details that tell about the first subject.
- In the right circle, write details that tell about the second subject.
- In the middle space, write details that tell how both subjects are the same.

Read these sentences. Compare and contrast Wilbur and Orville Wright.

Wilbur was born in 1867 in Milville, Indiana. Orville was born in 1871 in Dayton, Ohio. Both boys were raised in a loving home, filled with books.

Think About It

Wilbur

born in 1867 in Milville, Indiana

Both
raised in a loving home

Orville

born in 1871 in Dayton, Ohio

Scan and Skim

When you **scan and skim,** you read quickly to get an idea of what an article is about.

- First scan the article. Look at the title and any pictures. These features will help you learn the topic.
- Next, skim the article. Look for key words about the topic. These key words will give you an idea of what you will learn about the topic.

Read the story. Use the Reading Guide for tips. The tips will help you scan and skim and compare and contrast as you read.

Reading Guide

When you look at the title and the picture, what topic do you think you're going to read about? Look for key words in the article to get an idea of what you'll learn about the topic when you read.

What did the Wright brothers share? How else were they alike?

What details show you how Wilbur and Orville are different? What clue words help you notice these differences?

The Wright Brothers: Two People, Not One

Wilbur and Orville Wright built the first working airplane. On December 17, 1903, they made the first flight of a powered airplane. These were great **feats** by two special men. Yet people often talk about the Wright Brothers as if they were one person. The two men shared the same goal. However, they were different in many ways.

Wilbur was born in 1867 in Milville, Indiana. Orville was born in 1871 in Dayton, Ohio. The boys were raised in a loving home, filled with books. They were both bright. But Wilbur was the better student. He was quiet, thoughtful, and hardworking. He read all the time. He also liked doing research. On the other hand, Orville was full of energy. He loved adventure, but didn't always do his work. He sometimes got into trouble at school.

Later, Wilbur became a great writer and speaker. Orville became a **champion** bicycle rider. It was Wilbur who came up with the idea for the first airplane. It was Orville's energy that helped make that dream come true.

Now use what you learned to compare and contrast.

Answer the questions on the next page.

Practice the Skill 2

R3.3   Compare and contrast characters, plot, and setting in literary works, with assistance.

Practice comparing and contrasting by answering questions about the article you just read. Read each question. Circle the letter of the best answer.

1. What goal did Wilbur and Orville share?

   A Flying an airplane
   B Becoming champion bike riders
   C Writing a book
   D Doing research

2. According to the article, Wilbur and Orville —

   A were the same age
   B were born in different states
   C had the same hobbies
   D read the same books

3. Wilbur and Orville were both —

   A well-behaved at school
   B full of adventure
   C great speakers
   D bright children

4. Which of these is a word that describes Orville, but <u>not</u> Wilbur?

   A Hardworking
   B Energetic
   C Quiet
   D Thoughtful

5. Which of these statements is probably true?

   A Wilbur got better grades in school than Orville did.
   B Orville liked reading more than Wilbur did.
   C Wilbur got into trouble more often than Orville did.
   D Orville spent more time doing homework than Wilbur did.

6. On a separate sheet of paper, tell how Wilbur and Orville were alike and different. How did this help make their dream come true?

8-YEAR-OLD MOUNTAIN CLIMBER REACHES NEW HEIGHTS

Aidan Gold has climbed some of the world's tallest mountains.

BOTHELL, WA—Aidan Gold is only 8 years old, but he has already climbed some of the world's tallest mountains.

Aidan climbed his first mountain when he was 3 years old. He liked it so much that he has been climbing ever since. He finished a 4-month climb with his family not long ago. During the trip, he and his family traveled all over Europe and Asia. They climbed mountains that are almost 20,000 feet tall.

Aidan is smaller and lighter than other climbers. He is only 4 feet tall and weighs just 60 pounds. He doesn't let that slow him down, though. Aidan is like other climbers because he enjoys the challenge and the beautiful views. Aidan likes to tell stories of his adventures when he is not climbing mountains. He even won a story contest near his hometown of Bothell, Washington.

This 8-year-old will be climbing mountains for years to come. He has nowhere to go but up.

Write About It

On a separate sheet of paper, explain how Aidan is different from other mountain climbers. Also explain how Aidan is similar to other mountain climbers. Use details from the article to help you write your answer.

LADDERS to SUCCESS

LESSON
1
Comparing and
Contrasting

Show What You Learned

R3.3   Compare and contrast characters, plot, and setting in literary works, with assistance.

Read this article about machines. Then answer the questions on the next page.

THE MOST AMAZING MACHINE

What is the most amazing machine in the world?

Is it the jet plane? Jets are big, powerful machines. The wings of some jumbo jets weigh over 90,000 pounds! Some jets can travel more than 12,000 miles without landing. Huge engines help keep them in the air.

Maybe it's the computer. They are powerful machines, too. Unlike jets, they don't have engines to make them work. They have CPUs. That stands for central **processing** unit. The first computers were used in business to **compute,** or figure out lots of numbers. These giant machines took up the space of whole rooms. Only trained people could use them. Today's computers fit on a desk. Even young children can use them to write, draw, and send e-mails to friends.

Maybe you don't think the jet or the computer is the most amazing machine. Maybe you agree with people who think the most amazing machine in the world is the human body.

Like a jet, the human body has an engine. Its engine is the heart. But no one has to turn it on or plug it in. On its own, the heart pumps about 2,000 gallons of blood a day through the body. By the end of the day, that blood has gone about 12,000 miles. A jet needs more than one engine to travel that far!

The body has its own CPU, too. The body's CPU is the brain. Like a computer's CPU, the brain controls all of the body's actions. It does this by sending messages to body parts. It's kind of like e-mail, only faster.

The body is a different kind of machine. It's not built in a factory. It moves on two feet. And it grows! Best of all, it's yours. Take good care of it. Unlike other machines, you can't buy a new one in a store!

Read each question. Circle the letter of the best answer.

1. According to the author, which of these are most alike?

   A The heart and a computer

   B Jet engines and the brain

   C A computer's CPU and the brain

   D A computer's CPU and the heart

2. The author compares the human heart to —

   A a computer

   B a giant metal machine

   C a water pump

   D an engine

3. Compared to today's computers, the first computers were —

   A faster

   B easier to use

   C bigger

   D smarter

4. Unlike a jet, a computer has —

   A e-mail

   B a big, powerful machine

   C trained workers

   D a central processing unit

5. How is the human heart different from a jet engine and a computer's CPU?

   A The heart does not need to be turned on or plugged in.

   B The heart does not have as many parts.

   C The heart cannot work on its own.

   D The heart lasts longer and works harder than an engine or CPU.

6. The author compares how the brain controls parts of the body to —

   A taking a plane trip

   B sending e-mail messages

   C figuring out number problems

   D shopping

7. Which of these is <u>not</u> a detail that the author uses to show how the human body is different from other machines?

   A It isn't built in a factory.

   B It walks on two feet.

   C It grows.

   D It can feel.

8. On a separate sheet of paper, tell one way the human body is the same and one way it is different from another machine you know.

Show What You Know

W3.3   Use organizational patterns such as compare/contrast and time order for expository writing.

Before you begin this lesson, take this quiz to show what you know about sequence. Read this story about an art project. Then answer the questions.

JUAN'S MOBILE

Juan had to make a mobile for art class. He wanted his mobile to show stormy weather. The first thing he did was look for pictures in old magazines. He found a picture of dark clouds and cut it out. Then, he cut out a picture of a snowflake. After that, he cut out a picture of a man. The man was chasing his hat in the wind.

Next, Juan looked for storm words. He found the word *blizzard*. Then he found *hurricane*. The last word he found was *tornado*. Juan cut out the words. He pasted the words and then the pictures onto stiff pieces of cardboard. After that, Juan punched a hole in each piece of cardboard. Then, he cut six pieces of string. He cut each string a different length. Next, he tied a piece of string to each picture and each word. Finally, he tied the other end of the strings to a coat hanger. His mobile was finished.

Circle the letter of the best answer.

1. What is the first thing Juan did when he began his mobile?

    A He cut out words.

    B He looked for words.

    C He cut string.

    D He looked for pictures.

2. What did Juan do before he cut out the picture of a snowflake?

    A He chased after his hat.

    B He tied string to a hanger.

    C He cut out a picture of dark clouds.

    D He pasted words onto cardboard.

3. What happened right after Juan pasted the pictures?

    A He punched holes.

    B He cut the string.

    C He tied the string.

    D He pasted words.

4. Which word helps to show the last thing Juan did to make his mobile?

    A *After*

    B *Finally*

    C *Then*

    D *Next*

LADDERS to SUCCESS

LESSON

2

Understanding Sequence

Guided Instruction 1

W3.3   Use organizational patterns such as compare/contrast and time order for expository writing.

Sequence is the order in which events happen. Knowing the correct time order can help you understand what you read.

To understand sequence,

- Think about what happens first.
- Think about what happens next and what happens after that.
- Find the event that happens last.
- Look for clue words such as *first* and *next* to help you find sequence.

Read these sentences. Follow the sequence to tell the order in which the events happen.

The caterpillar needs food right away. First, it eats its eggshell. Then it munches on leaves. It eats and eats. It stops eating after it grows to be about two inches long.

Think About It

1. I think about what the caterpillar *does* first and what it *does* after that.

2. The words *first, then,* and *until* show the order in which things happen.

3. The first thing that happens is the caterpillar eats the eggshell. The second thing is the caterpillar munches on leaves. The last thing is the caterpillar grows to be about two inches long.

Visualize

When you **visualize,** you picture in your mind what you are reading.

- Carefully read the writer's description of what is happening.
- Use the details to form pictures in your mind.

Read the story. Use the Reading Guide for tips. The tips will help you visualize and understand sequence as you read.

Reading Guide

Use details to form pictures in your mind as soon as you start reading. This will help you follow each new step in the butterfly's life.

Think about what happens right after the caterpillar hatches from its egg. Look for clue words to help you keep track of what happens.

Look for other words that help you understand sequence.

Think about what happens last. Picture the monarch after its wings dry and get strong.

Such a Pretty Insect

One of the prettiest insects in the garden is the black and orange monarch butterfly. Monarchs don't start life pretty. In fact, they don't start life as butterflies. A monarch begins life as a tiny egg. After a few days, the egg hatches on a leaf. A tiny **larva,** or caterpillar, comes out.

The caterpillar needs food right away. First, it eats its eggshell. Then it munches on leaves. It eats and eats. It stops eating after it grows to be about two inches long. Now, it's ready to start the next stage of its life. First it looks for a good branch. Then it wraps itself up in a green case with gold specks. This case is a **pupa.**

The pupa hangs from the branch for about two weeks. Finally, an adult butterfly breaks out. At first, its wings are damp and weak. Soon, the wings dry. They get strong, and the monarch flies away.

Now use what you learned to understand sequence.

Answer the questions on the next page.

Practice the Skill 1

W3.3   Use organizational patterns such as compare/contrast and time order for expository writing.

Practice understanding sequence in the article you just read.

EXAMPLE

What is the first stage in the life of a monarch butterfly?

A butterfly

B caterpillar

C egg

D larva

Think about details that tell what happens in a monarch butterfly's life.

I see that the monarch butterfly takes different shapes during its life.

Look for clue words that tell when things happen in a monarch butterfly's life.

I see the word *begins*. I know *begins* means "starts." I form a picture in my head of the monarch starting life as a tiny *egg*.

Tell what happens first.

The monarch starts life as an egg.

Now read each question. Circle the letter of the best answer.

1. What is the first thing a caterpillar does after it hatches from the egg?

   A It eats leaves.

   B It grows wings.

   C It eats its shell.

   D It makes silk.

2. A caterpillar stops eating after it —

   A eats all the leaves on a tree

   B grows to about two inches

   C eats the eggshell

   D makes a pupa

3. What does a caterpillar do before it starts to make its pupa?

   A It looks for a branch.

   B It munches on a branch.

   C It wraps itself up.

   D It turns orange and black.

4. Right before the adult monarch flies away, it —

   A eats and eats

   B grows two inches

   C lays eggs on a leaf

   D waits for its wings to get strong

Bill Burns' dogs used a flashlight to help save him.

DOGS SAVE OWNER'S LIFE

CENTERTON, IN—It's a good thing Bill Burns had his dogs with him when he went for his walk. Otherwise, he might not be alive today.

Burns has an illness called **diabetes**. When he was walking with his two dogs, Dusty and Butch, he **collapsed**. What the dogs did next was amazing.

First, one dog lay across Burns to keep him warm. Then, the other dog held a flashlight in his mouth. The light shined out into the evening sky. Soon, a deputy close by saw the light. He followed it and found Burns lying on the ground. He also saw how Burns's dogs were trying to help him. The deputy got him to a hospital, where he stayed for four days.

Luckily, Burns got better. He is very thankful for his dogs. He thinks they are heroes.

Write About It

Now practice the skill. Use information from this news article. Retell this article using the graphic organizer below. Make sure your ideas are in the order they occurred in the story.

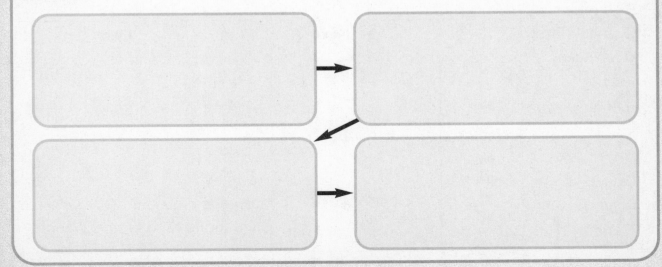

Ladder to Success

W3.3   Use organizational patterns such as compare/contrast and time order for expository writing.

Review

You have learned to think about what happens first, next, and last when you read. The order in which things happen is called **sequence.** As you read, you can put events in order to better understand what is happening in a story or article.

Review the steps you can use to understand sequence.

- Think about the order that things happen. Answer the questions, "What happens at the beginning?" "What happens in the middle?" "What happens at the end?"
- Look for time words that tell when things happen.
- Put events in order. Tell what happens first, next, and last.

Practice 1

Read the following story. As you read, think about what Rita sees from the swing. Pay attention to the order in which she sees each thing to understand sequence.

> Rita sat on the park swing. Signs of spring were all around. First, Rita saw a robin. It was busy building its nest. Then, Rita noticed that the giant piles of snow were gone. They had melted away. She saw that patches of bright green grass had taken their place. Finally, Rita saw a **clump** of flowers. Their pretty purple heads had pushed through the bare ground.

Using the sequence chart below, tell three different things Rita sees from the swing. Write them in the sequence that Rita sees them.

First	Next	Last

Practice 2

Read the passage. What is the sequence of events as Dave watches the sky turn from light to dark?

Dave watched night take over the sky. First, the clouds turned from white to smoky gray. Then, a star appeared. Dave didn't see it right away because the sky hadn't given up all its light yet. As soon as Dave spotted the first star, he closed his eyes and made a wish. By the time he opened his eyes again, a second star had appeared, and then a third. After a few minutes, the whole sky had turned a dark blue and was twinkling with stars. Dave shivered. The night had turned cold, and it was time to go inside.

Use this graphic organizer to show what happens in the story. Put the events in order from first to last to show sequence.

1.
2.
3.
4.

Practice 3

Read the passage. Follow the sequence of events to answer the questions. Make a graphic organizer on a separate sheet of paper to organize your thoughts.

Kim's day started terrible and got worse.

First, her alarm didn't go off. The night before, she had noticed the battery light blinking on her clock. So she went to the kitchen where her brother was making popcorn. Actually, he was burning it. Before Kim could ask her mom for batteries, the kitchen filled with smoke. Then the smoke alarm went off. After that, there was so much **commotion,** she forgot about the batteries.

Kim got up late and had to rush. When she went to the hall closet to get her sneakers, they weren't there. So she pulled on her old boots with the floppy right sole. Then she grabbed her schoolbag and ran to the bus stop. Of course, the floppy sole caught on the top step on the front porch and Kim fell. She didn't get hurt, but she did tear her jeans. She was about to go inside to change when her mother opened the front door.

"Guess you forgot," her mom said.

"Forgot what?" Kim asked.

"That today is Saturday," her mom said.

1. What is the first terrible thing of the day for Kim?

   _____

   _____

2. What two things happened before Kim had a chance to ask her mom for batteries?

   _____

   _____

3. What happened after Kim left the house in a rush?

   _____

   _____

LESSON

2

Understanding
Sequence

Guided Instruction 2

W3.3   Use organizational patterns such as compare/contrast and time order for expository writing.

Introduction

A writer uses **sequence** to help readers follow ideas in a story or article. A writer lists details and events in the order that will make the most sense to readers.

As you saw on pages 27–29, graphic organizers can help you understand sequence.

- Write a time or date on the left side of the time line. Start with the earliest date.
- Write a detail to go with that time or date in the space below.
- Write times or dates and details in time order from left to right across the time line.

Here's How

Read these sentences. How does understanding sequence help you follow events in Jim Henson's life?

Jim Henson was born in Mississippi in 1936. Around 1946, his family moved to Maryland. As a boy, Jim loved art. Television was a new idea back then. In 1954, when Jim was still in high school, he got his very first TV job.

Think About It

Date: 1936	**Date:** around 1946	**Date:** 1954
Detail: Jim Henson is born in Mississippi.	**Detail:** Jim and his family move to Maryland.	**Detail:** Jim gets his first TV job.

Try This Strategy

Summarize

When you **summarize,** you retell what happens in a story or article, but in a much shorter way and in your own words.

- As you read, look for the most important details, ideas, and events.
- Tell what happens at the beginning, in the middle, and at the end of what you read.
- Use your own words. Leave out details that are not important.

Read the story. Use the Reading Guide for tips. The tips will help you summarize and understand sequence as you read.

Reading Guide

Why is 1969 an important date in Jim Henson's life? Pay attention to other important dates in the article.

What happened to Jim while he was still in school? What time words and details does the writer use to help you follow the sequence of these events?

What events would you use to retell this whole article? Think about time words that could show the order in which events happened in Jim Henson's life.

The Muppet Master

Can you picture a world without Muppets? Wouldn't the world be much less yellow without Big Bird and much less green without Kermit?

Before 1969, only a few people had heard of Muppets. Then *Sesame Street* came on the air. Everyone wanted to know who had created the Muppets.

Jim Henson was born in Mississippi in 1936. Around 1946, his family moved to Maryland. As a boy, Jim loved art. Television was a new idea back then. In 1954, when Jim was still in high school, he got his very first TV job. He appeared on a children's show with puppets he had made. One of those puppets was named Pierre the French Rat.

The next year, Jim went to college. While he was there, he got his own TV show, *Sam and Friends*. The show starred Jim's puppets, called Muppets. One of those Muppets was a frog, who later became a big star.

By 1963, Jim and his Muppets had been guests on many TV shows. Then, in 1966, a woman named Joan Cooney asked Jim to make Muppets for a new children's show. That show was *Sesame Street*.

The Muppets are now part of TV history.

Now use what you learned to understand sequence.

Answer the questions on the next page.

Practice the Skill 2

W3.3   Use organizational patterns such as compare/contrast and time order for expository writing.

Practice understanding sequence by answering questions about the article you just read. Read each question. Circle the letter of the best answer.

1. According to the article, everyone wanted to know about Jim Henson and the Muppets after —

   A *Sam and Friends* began

   B *Sesame Street* came on the air

   C Jim performed with Pierre the French Rat

   D Jim started college

2. Jim Henson's puppet characters first appeared on television in —

   A 1969

   B 1946

   C 1966

   D 1954

3. What happened before Jim got out of high school?

   A He got his own TV show.

   B He was asked to make Muppets for a new TV show.

   C He got a job on a TV show.

   D He moved to Maryland.

4. Which of these events happened first?

   A Jim Henson makes his first Muppets.

   B Jim Henson's Muppets appear on *Sesame Street*.

   C Joan Cooney asks Jim Henson to make Muppets for a new TV show.

   D Kermit the frog becomes a big star.

5. Before 1963, Jim Henson and the Muppets —

   A were totally unknown

   B appeared as guests on many TV shows

   C were loved by children and adults everywhere

   D appeared on *Sesame Street* many times

6. On a separate sheet of paper, summarize the important events in Jim Henson's life that show how he became famous. Use your own words and be sure to tell events in the order they happened.

Phil Says, "SIX MORE WEEKS OF WINTER!"

Punxsutawney Phil has predicted six more weeks of winter nearly 100 times.

PUNXSUTAWNEY, PA—As the sun rose on February 2, Punxsutawney Phil gave his forecast. It's **official.** There will be six more weeks of winter, he predicted.

Every February 2 is Groundhog Day. Early in the morning, a huge crowd gathers at Gobbler's Knob. But they don't just wait in the dark. People enjoy music, games, and fireworks. Then at sunrise, Phil the groundhog comes out of his hole. Next, he checks if he can see his shadow. If he sees it, there will be six more weeks of winter. If he does not, spring will come early.

After Phil checks for his shadow, he gives his weather prediction in his own language. It's called "Groundhogese." The president of the Groundhog Club **translates** Phil's words into English. Then he reads Phil's message to the crowd.

Most groundhogs live six to eight years. But Phil is given a magical Groundhog Punch every summer. It adds seven years to his life. Phil is now more than 120 years old!

Phil has become famous. He has been on TV and in movies. He has his own website. He knows famous actors and musicians. And he has even visited the White House to meet a president! Phil's special day is February 2, but he's busy all year!

Write About It

Now you will practice the skill using a real news story. On a separate sheet of paper, explain how Punxsutawney Phil makes a prediction. Include at least three things he does and the order he does them in.

LADDERS to SUCCESS

LESSON
2
Understanding
Sequence

Show What You Learned

W3.3   Use organizational patterns such as compare/contrast and time order for expository writing.

Read this story about a lizard and her tail. Then answer the questions on the next page.

Lizzie's Tail

Lizzie Lizard leaped out of bed. The first thing she did was wiggle her colorful tail. Lizzie was proud of her tail, but she also had another reason to be happy. Exactly three months ago, she had hatched. She hoped her desert friends were planning a surprise hatchday party for her. "I can't wait," she said.

Lizzie crawled from her dark burrow into the bright light of the Texas sun. She began looking for some yummy bugs for breakfast. After Lizzie had eaten, she climbed on top of a rock to nap. Suddenly, a dark shadow hovered over her. It was her enemy, the **raptor** Rap.

The large bird swooped down and tried to capture Lizzie. She scooted away, running down and under the rock. On the way, Lizzie bumped her tail. "Oh, no!" she cried. A piece of her tail had broken off. Lizzie began to sob loudly.

"Who's making that racket?" someone hollered. Lizzie peeked out from under the rock. It was her friend, Squeak, the deer mouse.

"I broke my tail," Lizzie howled. "It was supposed to be such a wonderful day, but now it's absolutely ruined."

"Relax," Squeak said. "It's not the end of the world."

"Yes, it is," Lizzie said. "My tail helps me move. How will I find food? How will I escape from Rap? And watch what happens when I try to lift my head." Lizzie tumbled over onto her side. She began to cry again.

"Your tail will **regenerate,**" Squeak said as he helped Lizzie up.

"What does that mean?" Lizzie cried.

"It means your tail will grow back," answered Squeak.

Lizzie asked through her tears. "But how will I survive until then?"

"I'll help you," Squeak said.

Finally, Lizzie stopped crying. "Thanks," she said.

"It's nothing," Squeak said. "Now, cheer up, because we've got a party to get to!"

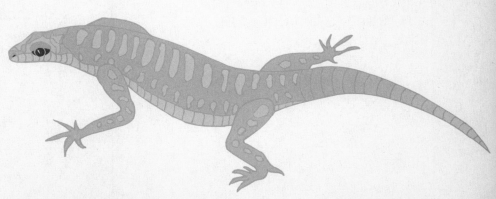

Read each question. Circle the letter of the best answer.

1. Which of these events happens before the story begins?

   A Lizzie hides under a rock.

   B Lizzie breaks her tail.

   C Lizzie hatches.

   D Lizzie plans a party.

2. What is the first thing Lizzie does after she leaps out of bed?

   A She wiggles her tail.

   B She climbs on a rock.

   C She looks for bugs.

   D She talks to a friend.

3. The first thing Lizzie sees after she crawls from her burrow is —

   A Rap

   B Squeak

   C bright sunlight

   D her broken tail

4. Before Lizzie sees Rap's shadow, she is —

   A crying about her tail

   B about to take a nap

   C planning a surprise party

   D trying to find Squeak

5. Which of these events does not happen after Lizzie sees Rap's shadow?

   A Lizzie scoots away.

   B Lizzie runs under a rock.

   C Lizzie bumps her tail.

   D Lizzie eats breakfast.

6. In the story, which event happens after Lizzie breaks her tail?

   A She eats breakfast.

   B She tries to lift her head and falls over.

   C A shadow hovers over her.

   D She takes a nap on a sunny rock.

7. Lizzie finally stops crying after Squeak tells her —

   A that her tail will grow back

   B that it's not the end of the world

   C that it's time to go to a party

   D that he will help her

8. On a separate sheet of paper, write three things that happened to Lizzie before she broke her tail. Write the events in the order they happened. Use time words to show sequence.

Show What You Know

R3.LC   Organize and categorize text information by using knowledge of a variety of text structures (e.g., cause and effect, fact and opinion, directions, time sequence).

Before you begin this lesson, take this quiz to show what you know about cause and effect. Read this story. Then answer the questions.

SAVING SUMMER

Every summer, Kelsey and her friend Marcy looked forward to two things: the carnival and the parade. This year the mayor called off the carnival. Kelsey couldn't understand why.

"Miss Gregory owns the dance studio. She doesn't want the public parking lot used for the carnival." Mom said. "Her students and workers park there. If that lot is closed, she'll have to cancel classes. Then she'll lose money."

Dad looked up from the newspaper. "More bad news," he said. "The mayor is also canceling the parade. The money from the carnival pays for the parade. No carnival, no parade." Kelsey felt so sad. She went to her room and threw herself on her bed.

The next day, Kelsey's dad had better news. "Marcy's dad owns a parking garage downtown," he said. "He's going to let people use his parking garage for free. So Miss Gregory can stay open. And since the carnival is back on, we'll get our parade, too."

"Yay! Kelsey yelled. "Summer is saved!"

Circle the letter of the best answer.

1. Why was the carnival canceled?

  A The carnival was the same day as the parade.

  B Miss Gregory didn't want the public parking lot closed.

  C The mayor didn't like it.

  D Marcy's father wouldn't let workers use his garage.

2. What would happen as a result of canceling the carnival?

  A The parade would be cancelled.

  B The mayor would lose the election.

  C They would have the parade.

  D Miss Gregory would lose money.

3. How did Marcy's dad save summer?

  A He paid for the carnival.

  B He signed Kelsey and Marcy up for dance classes.

  C He helped Miss Gregory and the mayor come to an agreement.

  D He let people use his garage for free, so the carnival could be held.

4. Kelsey was sad because —

  A she was tired from the carnival

  B she was mad at her parents

  C she thought summer was ruined

  D she was practicing for dance class

<table>
<tr><td>LADDERS
to SUCCESS
LESSON
3
Recognizing Cause
and Effect</td></tr>
</table>

Guided Instruction 1

R3.LC   Organize and categorize text information by using knowledge of a variety of text structures (e.g., cause and effect, fact and opinion, directions, time sequence).

Introduction

Events in a story or passage often happen for a reason. A **cause** makes something happen. What happens as a result is the **effect.** When you read, think about what happens and why it happens.

To recognize cause and effect,

- Look for details that tell what happened.
- To find the cause of an event, ask yourself, "Why did this happen?" Clue words such as *because* and *since* can help you find the cause.
- To find an effect, think of what happened because of the event. Clue words such as *so* and *result* can help you find an effect.

Here's How

Read these sentences. Look for what causes the caterpillars to grow and change.

Because those caterpillars fill up on tasty treats in your closet, they grow and change. Soon, they turn into moths.

Think About It

1. Caterpillars *eat* things, *grow* and *change*, and *turn* into moths.

2. I am looking for the *cause* for caterpillars growing and changing. I ask myself: "Why *does* this happen?"

3. I *see* the word *because*. This tells me that filling up on tasty treats is the cause of caterpillars' growing and changing.

Try This Strategy

Monitor and Clarify

You **monitor and clarify** to make sure you understand what you read.

- After reading each paragraph, pause and think about the main ideas. Try to restate them in your own words. Try to clarify *why* things happen.
- If you did not understand the main ideas, reread the paragraph.

Read the story. Use the Reading Guide for tips. The tips will help you monitor and clarify and recognize cause and effect as you read.

Reading Guide

When you wonder why something happened, you are looking for a cause.

Look for clue words, such as so *and* because.

If you don't understand the causes and effects in this paragraph, reread carefully. Restate the key ideas in your own words.

A Meal for a Caterpillar

Have you ever found a hole your sweater? You may have wondered, "How did that get there?" You know you didn't catch it on a nail. It didn't have a hole in it when you put it away.

The **culprit** may have been a moth. Actually, moths don't eat sweaters. A sweater is warm and soft, so it's a good place for a moth to lay eggs. When those eggs hatch, very hungry caterpillars come out of them. Because they are so hungry, they need something to eat right away.

These caterpillars love to eat wool, silk, and fur. These materials all come from animals. For some reason, caterpillars don't usually eat **fibers** that come from plants. They also don't like man-made fibers such as polyester.

Because those caterpillars fill up on tasty treats in your closet, they grow and change. Soon, they turn into moths. You should try to catch them as soon as they become moths. If not, they will lay eggs. Then the eggs will hatch, causing the whole hungry cycle to start again!

Now use what you learned to recognize cause and effect.

Answer the questions on the next page.

Practice the Skill 1

R3.LC   Organize and categorize text information by using knowledge of a variety of text structures (e.g., cause and effect, fact and opinion, directions, time sequence).

Practice recognizing cause and effect in the passage you just read.

EXAMPLE

Why is a sweater a good place for moths to lay eggs?

A A sweater is made by a machine.

B A sweater is warm and soft.

C A sweater grows and changes.

D A sweater is stored in a closet.

Look for details that tell you what happens.

I reread the second paragraph, and I see that moths lay eggs in sweaters. I see that sweaters are described as warm and soft.

Think about the event and why it happens.

I ask myself, "Why does this happen?"

Look for clue words that show a cause.

I see the clue word *so*. This tells me that moths lay eggs in sweaters because a sweater is warm and soft. This is the cause.

Now read each question. Circle the letter of the best answer.

1. Because new-born caterpillars are very hungry they —

    A need to eat right away

    B grow huge, then change

    C don't eat man-made fibers

    D fight for space with moths

2. According to the passage, how did you get a hole in your sweater?

    A It is made with plant fibers.

    B You caught it on a nail.

    C You forgot to get rid of the moths in your closet.

    D You tore it by accident.

3. Why do caterpillars eat wool sweaters?

    A They are very hungry.

    B They need to be warm.

    C They need to lay eggs.

    D They like plant fibers.

4. Why is it good to get rid of moths in your closet?

    A They'll eat your sweaters.

    B They'll grow and change.

    C They'll lay more eggs.

    D They'll die quickly.

Go to SCHOOL, Win a PRIZE

Some schools are rewarding attendance with new bikes.

ROSSVILLE, GA—Going to school is fun for Scott Daniels. He won a new bike there. He won the bike because he went to school every day.

Many kids are earning rewards for going to school. Attendance is important. As a result, principals and teachers are asking, "How can we **convince** kids to come to school every day?" In some towns, rewards are the answer.

Schools use different kinds of rewards. Some schools add points to grades. Others give movie tickets or T-shirts.

Some people say rewards are a good idea. Others complain because they think rewards send a bad message about learning.

Even if they send a bad message, rewards work because kids want the prizes. They caused Scott Daniels to go to school every day. In fact, attendance is up at Daniels's school. Test scores are up, too!

Write About It

Now practice the skill. Use information from this news article. Fill in the graphic organizer. Write one cause you read about. Then write the effect.

Cause	Effect

LADDERS to SUCCESS

LESSON

3

Recognizing Cause and Effect

R3.LC   Organize and categorize text information by using knowledge of a variety of text structures (e.g., cause and effect, fact and opinion, directions, time sequence).

Ladder to Success

Review

You have learned how to **recognize cause and effect.** A **cause** is what makes something happen. The **effect** is what happens as a result of the cause.

Review the steps you can use to recognize cause and effect.

- Read to find details about what happens.
- To find the cause of something, think about why it happened. Look for clue words, such as *because* or *since*.
- To find an effect, think of what happened as a result of the event. Look for clue words, such as *so* or *as a result*.

Practice 1

Read the following passage. As you read, think about the events. Ask yourself why Washington, D.C. looks the way it does. Look for clue words to help you find a cause.

> When the nation's capital, Washington, D.C., was first planned, it was a square. Each side was 10 miles long. The square used land from Maryland and Virginia. In the mid-1800s, Virginia decided to take back its part of land. So all the land south and west of the Potomac River was returned to Virginia. That's why today, instead of a square, Washington, D.C. looks more like a sandwich with a big bite taken out of it!

Complete the graphic organizer below to show cause and effect from the passage.

Cause	Effect
	Today, instead of a square, Washington, D.C. looks more like a sandwich with a big bite taken out of it.

Practice 2

Read the passage. What causes and effects does the writer explain?

Take a deep breath and blow out. If the air outside is cold, you'll see your breath. Do you know why? The air that comes out of your lungs is warm, like your body, and it has some water **vapor** in it. Your body is warm, and so is your breath. Your breath is made up of water vapor. When the warm, moist air of your breath hits the cold air outside, the water vapor in your breath cools quickly. As a result, the water vapor condenses, or gets squeezed together. When water vapor condenses, tiny water droplets form. This is the same process that makes clouds form. Water vapor in the Earth's atmosphere cools and condenses. So, on a cold day, you can make "clouds" just by breathing!

Fill in this graphic organizer to recognize causes and effects.

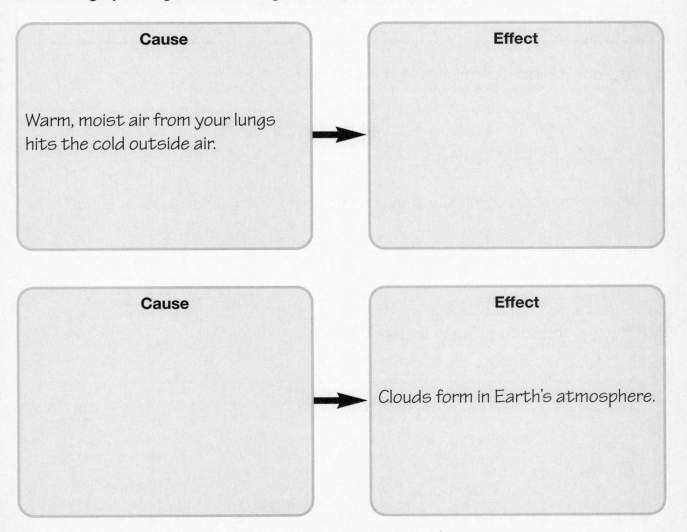

Cause	Effect
Warm, moist air from your lungs hits the cold outside air.	

Cause	Effect
	Clouds form in Earth's atmosphere.

Practice 3

Read the passage. Then answer the questions by recognizing cause and effect. On a separate sheet of paper, make a graphic organizer to organize your thoughts.

Hoshi thought the kites were amazing. He could spot Uncle Jiro easily in the crowd because of his bright red shirt. He was one of the best players in the contest. The kites flew like fighter planes in old war movies. High up in the sky, they danced on the wind. They looked beautiful. However, Hoshi knew they were dangerous. Each kite's string was coated in sand, ground glass, or bits of metal. As a result, players can cut the enemy kites out of the sky.

Fifty kites had started the battle hours ago. There would be only one winner. Hoshi hoped it would be Uncle Jiro. Uncle Jiro was one of the final two kites left in the battle. It was going to be a tough finish because the last two flyers were **experts.** Suddenly, Uncle Jiro's kite was snapped from its line. Hoshi felt sad watching the kite sail to the ground. It was finally over.

1. Why could Hoshi spot his uncle in the crowd?

   _____

   _____

2. What is the effect of the kite strings being coated with sand, glass, or metal?

   _____

   _____

3. Why was the finish going to be tough?

   _____

   _____

Guided Instruction 2

R3.LC Organize and categorize text information by using knowledge of a variety of text structures (e.g., cause and effect, fact and opinion, directions, time sequence).

Introduction

To **recognize cause and effect,** you need to think about what happens and why it happens. What happens is the **effect.** Why it happens is the **cause.**

As you saw on pages 41–43, graphic organizers can help you recognize cause and effect.

- Think about what happens. Read to find out why it happens.
- Write what happens in the *Effect* box.
- Write why it happens in the *Cause* box.

Here's How

Read these sentences. Rosie knew all the answers. What was the result, or the effect?

The next day was the test. Rosie was ready. She picked up her pencil and zipped through it. Since she knew all the answers, she was sure she'd get 100 percent.

Think About It

Cause	Effect
Rosie knew all the answers.	She was sure she'd get 100 percent.

Try This Strategy

Visualize

When you **visualize,** you form a picture in your mind.

- As you read, think about how the writer describes what happens.
- Use the description to form a mental picture.
- Imagine the things that happen as if they were taking place in a movie in your mind.

Read the story. Use the Reading Guide for tips. The tips will help you visualize and recognize cause and effect as you read.

Reading Guide

How do the clue words why *and* if *help you recognize causes and effects in this paragraph?*

Visualize the series of events the writer describes. Can you picture each cause and each effect?

What details help you understand what the characters said and did, and why?

THE FLAG TEST

Rosie was tired of coming in third in the American flag contest. That's why she needed her mom to test her. Mr. Hackett had given the students a list of flag facts. If Rosie memorized them all, she'd get 100 percent and win that flag!

Mom had found another list of important flag dates in Rosie's book bag. Mr. Hackett hadn't said those dates would be on the test, so Rosie wasn't going to study them. But Mom believed if there was something to learn, you should learn it. Rosie knew she wouldn't win this battle, so she let her mom quiz her on the dates.

The next day was the test. Rosie was ready. She picked up her pencil and zipped through it. Since she knew all the answers, she was sure she'd get 100 percent. Then Rosie turned to the last page of the test. Across the top, it said "Extra Credit." Rosie read the questions. Every single one was about the dates her mom had made her memorize. Rosie smiled, quickly filled in all of the answers, and handed the test in.

Now use what you learned to recognize cause and effect.

Answer the questions on the next page.

Practice the Skill 2

Practice recognizing cause and effect. Answer questions about the story you just read. Read each question. Circle the letter of the best answer.

1. Why did Rosie want her mom to test her?

    A She didn't want to win the flag that year.

    B Her mom knew everything about the American flag.

    C Mr. Hackett had said it would be a good idea.

    D She was tired of coming in third in the contest.

2. Rosie knew that the result of memorizing the flag facts would be —

    A she would come in third again and have to wait another year

    B she would have more time to study for other tests

    C she would get 100 percent on the test and win the flag

    D she would be able to skip the test completely

3. Rosie knew she wouldn't win the battle with her mother, so she —

    A let her mom quiz her on the other list of dates

    B didn't answer "Extra Credit" questions

    C asked Mr. Hackett for extra help

    D memorized only the list of dates

4. Why wasn't Rosie going to study the list of dates?

    A Her mother didn't want her to spend her time on that.

    B Mr. Hackett hadn't said the dates would be on the test.

    C She wanted to be surprised by the test questions.

    D She didn't care whether she did well on the flag test.

5. Which statement from the passage tells why Rosie zipped through the test?

    A *She picked up her pencil.*

    B *Rosie smiled.*

    C *Rosie was ready.*

    D *Rosie was tired.*

6. Why did Rosie smile when she saw the last page of the test? Write your answer on a separate sheet of paper.

Siblings Win GOLD MEDALS

Brothers Steven and Mark Lopez, along with their sister Diana, won Taekwondo medals.

HOUSTON, TX—Now that's a talented family! Three siblings each won a gold medal at the Taekwondo World Championships in Spain recently. Steven, Mark, and Diana Lopez were the first three siblings to win at a world championship event.

Steven, the oldest, was the first to win a gold medal. It was his third straight year as Taekwondo champion. Diana, the youngest, won her gold medal just two days later. Mark, the middle sibling, won his gold medal the same day. He was able to watch his sister win just before his own fight began.

Taekwondo is a fighting style that started in Korea. It is known for its fast, high-spinning kicks.

The Lopez siblings trained for the championships at the Elite Taekwondo Center near their home in Houston. Their older brother, Jean, runs the center. Jean coached his siblings to their record-breaking wins.

Write About It

Now you will practice the skill using a real news story. On a separate sheet of paper, write what may have caused three kids from the same family to fight in the same sport.

LADDERS to SUCCESS

LESSON
3
Recognizing Cause
and Effect

Show What You Learned

R3.LC   Organize and categorize text information by using knowledge of a variety of text structures (e.g., cause and effect, fact and opinion, directions, time sequence).

Read this article about an unusual flood. Then answer the questions on the next page.

The Great Molasses Flood

Most floods are caused by too much rain. Sometimes, too much rain fills rivers, and the rivers overflow their banks. Other times, too much rain fills lakes or **reservoirs.** This can cause dams or other walls to break and the water to rush out. Every once in a while, though, a flood is caused by something entirely different from rain. Sometimes a flood isn't even caused by water.

On January 15, 1919, a **molasses** tank in Boston, Massachusetts, burst. Over two million gallons of heated molasses flowed through the streets of Boston in a thick wave. Everything was covered with the hot, sugary syrup. Horses and cars were stuck in it. The sewers were clogged. Many homes were destroyed. Some homes were crushed by the twenty-foot wall of molasses, and many others were ruined when rooms filled with the sticky goop.

The city tried to clean up the mess with freshwater from hydrants, but the water had no effect. The city ended up using water from the harbor. When the salty water was sprayed on the molasses, the molasses began to dissolve. It took half a year to clean the streets. As a result of the molasses being washed into it, Boston Harbor turned brown for six months.

It's not known exactly what caused the disaster. Some people believe the tank was overfilled, causing it to crack open. Others think that the weather was the cause. The day before, the outside temperature was only 2°F. On the day of the flood, the temperature rose unexpectedly to 40°F. Since the temperature rose so fast, the molasses could have warmed up too quickly. A result of this could have been that the molasses expanded and broke open the tank.

Sadly, 21 people died in the disaster, known as the Great Molasses Flood. Some people claim that on a hot day, even now, you can still smell the molasses.

Read each question. Circle the letter of the best answer.

1. What causes most floods?

   A Temperature changes
   B Unexpected heat waves
   C Too much rain
   D Overfilled reservoirs

2. What can happen when too much rain fills up a river?

   A Dams break.
   B A river overflows its banks.
   C Houses are crushed by waves.
   D Freshwater flows into the harbor.

3. What is the effect when a dam breaks?

   A Water rushes out.
   B Large tanks burst.
   C Molasses fills the streets.
   D The harbor turns brown.

4. What was the result when the molasses tank burst?

   A Horses and people ran from the city.
   B Over two million gallons of hot molasses flooded the streets of Boston.
   C The freshwater hydrants no longer worked as they were supposed to.
   D The molasses expanded rapidly.

5. What caused the houses to be destroyed?

   A Horses ran inside and ruined the furniture.
   B Salt water was sprayed on them.
   C They were washed into the harbor.
   D They were crushed by the wave of molasses.

6. What happened when salt water was sprayed on the molasses?

   A The molasses dissolved.
   B The molasses was not affected.
   C It made the molasses sticky.
   D The molasses became warm.

7. Why did Boston Harbor turn brown for six months?

   A Dirty hydrant water was poured into it.
   B The temperature rose too quickly.
   C The molasses got into it.
   D It was overfilled by rainwater.

8. The article describes two possible causes for the Great Molasses Flood. Choose one and explain it on a separate sheet of paper.

Show What You Know

R3.LC   Learn new vocabulary and concepts indirectly by reading books and other print sources.

Before you begin this lesson, take this quiz to show what you know about using context clues. Read this story about a turtle and his friends. Then answer the questions.

SUCH A FUSS!

Snap sat on the rock near the woodpile. "How <u>bizarre</u>!" he thought. "How strange!"

Squirrel was running in circles. Her tail was spinning faster and faster. She looked like a <u>tornado</u>, one of those twisting windstorms that Snap had heard about.

Bunny was hopping up and down like a wild rabbit. She looked like she could hop to the moon and back.

Crow was cawing from high in the tree. What a <u>racket</u> he was making! The noise hurt Snap's ears, so he pulled his head into his shell. It didn't help.

Snap pushed his head out again. "Will someone tell me what's going on?" he said. Snake crawled next to him on the rock.

"They're excited," Snake hissed. "Mama Skunk has a new baby. There's the cute little <u>kit</u> now."

Snap looked at the baby skunk. She was sweet-looking, but Snap didn't think they should all be making such a fuss. But then, turtles are always calm.

Circle the letter of the best answer.

1. What word in the first paragraph of the story gives a clue to the meaning of <u>bizarre</u>?

    A *rock*

    B *near*

    C *thought*

    D *strange*

2. From the clues in the passage, you can tell that a <u>tornado</u> is —

    A a squirrel

    B a windstorm

    C a hissing snake

    D a circle

3. To make a <u>racket</u> means —

    A to jump up and down

    B to spin in circles

    C to be very noisy

    D to hide in a shell

4. Which words explain the meaning of <u>kit</u> in the story?

    A *baby skunk*

    B *wild rabbit*

    C *on the rock*

    D *tree*

Guided Instruction 1

R3.LC   Learn new vocabulary and concepts indirectly by reading books and other print sources.

When you read, you may find words you don't know. **Context clues** are words you *do* know that help you figure out the meaning of words you *don't* know. A context clue may be a word that has the same meaning. It may be a word that means the opposite. Or it may explain what the word means.

To use context clues,

- Reread the sentence with the new word. Read the sentences that come before and after that sentence.
- Look in those sentences for clues that explain the meaning of the new word. Check for synonyms or opposites. Check for words that explain.

Here's How

Read these sentences. What context clues can tell you what <u>stern</u> means?

Pete, the camp leader, gathered campers together. Earlier, Pete had been making jokes. But now he was <u>stern</u>. "It's a bad idea to store food in your tent," Pete said.

Think About It

1. I reread the sentence with the word <u>stern</u>.

2. The sentence before tells me that Pete had been making jokes. The next sentence begins with *but,* which tells when something is the opposite.

3. I think <u>stern</u> is the opposite of making jokes. It means "serious."

Try This Strategy

Use Prior Knowledge

When you **use prior knowledge,** you use what you know to understand a story.

- Read about the story characters and what happens to them. Think about how they are like people and events you know.
- Combine what you read and know to understand what happens in the story.

Read the story. Use the Reading Guide for tips. The tips will help you use prior knowledge and context clues as you read.

Reading Guide

Look for context clues that help you understand the meaning of <u>snack</u>. Look for words in the same sentence that could be examples of a snack.

Look for context clues that help you understand the meaning of <u>attract</u>. Notice the words keep them out.

Look for context clues in sentences around <u>peek</u> that can help you figure out its meaning. Notice what Jon is doing. Notice that Rosie and Kenny are doing that, too.

Jon's First Camping Trip

Pete, the camp leader, gathered campers together. Earlier, Pete had been making jokes. But now he was stern. "It's a bad idea to store food in your tent," Pete said.

"Why?" Jon asked. Jon liked to have a small <u>snack</u> before bed, like pretzels and apples.

"We're in bear country," Pete said. "Bears have a <u>powerful</u> sense of smell. It's so strong, they can <u>sniff</u> food from far away. We don't want to <u>attract</u> bears into our tents. We want to keep them out."

That night, Jon was almost asleep when he heard a noise. He looked outside his tent. He saw his friends Rosie and Kenny <u>peek</u> out of their tents, too. Rosie pointed to a dark shadow near the trees. It was a bear!

Seconds later, food came flying out of the tents. Candy, pretzels, apples, cupcakes—it was like a grocery store had exploded.

The bear grabbed the food and left. None of us kept food in our tents after that.

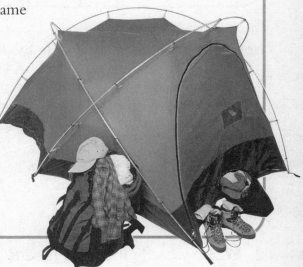

Now use what you learned to use context clues.

Answer the questions on the next page.

LADDERS to SUCCESS

LESSON
4
Using Context Clues

Practice the Skill 1

R3.LC   Learn new vocabulary and concepts indirectly by reading books and other print sources.

Practice using context clues in the story you just read.

EXAMPLE

In the story, the word <u>sniff</u> probably means —

A to camp

B to smell

C to eat

D to sleep

Read the sentence with the new word again. Read the sentences around the word.

I read the sentence with the word <u>sniff</u> and the sentences around it.

Find clues that help you understand what the word means.

I see the words *sense of smell* in the sentence that comes before the sentence with <u>sniff</u>.

Tell the meaning of the new word.

I think <u>sniff</u> means "to smell."

Now read each question. Circle the letter of the best answer.

1. Which words in the story give a clue to the meaning of <u>snack</u>?

   A *camp leader*

   B *pretzels* and *apples*

   C *bear country*

   D *before bed*

2. Which word in the story means almost the same as <u>powerful</u> and is a clue to the meaning of powerful?

   A *funny*

   B *small*

   C *strong*

   D *dark*

3. From the clues in the story, you can tell that <u>attract</u> means —

   A to send away

   B to find

   C to look like

   D to pull toward

4. In this story, the best meaning for <u>peek</u> is —

   A to look

   B to eat

   C to point

   D to fly

A NASA hot-air balloon floated in space for 41 days.

MCMURDO STATION, ANTARCTICA—
How do we learn about space? One way is by using balloons. Huge balloons fly near the edge of outer space. They collect <u>data</u>, or information. They help us learn about rays, gases, and more.

One balloon broke all records. The huge hot-air balloon floated at the edge of space for almost six weeks. It <u>orbited</u>, or went around, the South Pole three times.

In the past, balloons stayed in the air about two weeks. In 2002, a balloon stayed in the air for over four weeks. Six weeks is a new record.

The balloons are filled with helium. Helium is a gas that can cause things to float in the air. Sunlight also helps keep balloons in the air.

BALLOON BREAKS RECORD

Write About It

Now practice the skill. Use information from this news article. Fill in the chart. Write the context clues that help you understand each word. The first one is done for you.

New Word	Clues	Meaning
data	*or information*	information
orbited		

LADDERS to SUCCESS

LESSON

4

Using Context Clues

Ladder to Success

R3.LC   Learn new vocabulary and concepts indirectly by reading books and other print sources.

Review

When you come across new or unfamiliar words, look for **context clues.** Synonyms, opposites, and words that explain are context clues. Finding context clues can help you understand the meaning of new words.

Review the steps for using context clues.

- If you come to a word you don't know, reread the sentence.
- Look for context clues within the sentence that might tell about the word.
- Read the sentences that come before and after that sentence. Look for context clues here, too.
- Think about what the context clues mean.
- Apply the meaning of the context clues to figure out the meaning of the word.

Practice 1

Read the following passage. As you read, look for context clues to help you learn the meaning of <u>argument</u>. Look for a word that means the same. Pay attention to the meaning of all the sentences. Use all the context clues to figure out the meaning of <u>argument</u>.

> Sun and Wind got into a big <u>argument</u>. Their fight went on for a long time. "I'm stronger than you," Sun said. "No. I'm stronger," Wind said. One day, Sun and Wind found a way to prove who was stronger. They saw a man walking down the road. The first one to make the man take off his coat would win. The sun hid behind a cloud. Wind began to blow very hard. He blew harder and harder. The man pulled his coat tighter to stay warm. Then Sun came back out. He shined as bright as could be. The man got so hot, he took off his coat.

Fill in the chart below. Show how you used context clues to figure out the meaning of <u>argument</u>.

New Word	Context Clues	Your Meaning
argument		

Practice 2

Read the passage. What context clues help you figure out the meanings of the underlined words?

There was a <u>fascinating</u> new thing in Mr. Snow's junk shop window. Every day, Lenny and Dave came and stared at it. Then each of them would guess what it was.

So far they had made some funny guesses. Lenny had guessed it was a hat for dogs to make them smarter. Dave had guessed it was the first <u>automatic</u> dishwasher. "You press that button on the side," he said. "And those metal arms wash the dishes in a snap."

One day, Mr. Snow came out of the shop. "I can tell you boys what that is," he said.

"No thanks," they said together. "What fun would that be?"

Fill in this graphic organizer. Show how context clues helped you to find the meanings of the underlined words.

New Word	Context Clues	Your Meaning
fascinating		
automatic		

Practice 3

Read the passage. Then use context clues to answer the questions. Make a graphic organizer on a separate sheet of paper to organize your thoughts.

> Most mother ducks lay their eggs in a <u>marsh</u>. Wet, grassy places are perfect for nesting. When the eggs hatch, the mother and the father can easily find food for their ducklings. They can also teach them to swim.
>
> One light brown duck from Washington, D.C. found an unusual spot to nest. She laid her eggs in a planter outside the Ritz-Carlton hotel in Georgetown. Mother Duck, as people call her, has good taste. The Ritz is a fancy hotel.
>
> Mother Duck padded her nest with <u>down</u>, or soft duck feathers. Then she laid 11 eggs. Hotel workers watched over the nest day and night. While Mother Duck was nesting, the hotel restaurant took duck off the menu. It just didn't seem right.
>
> Then, it was time for the eggs to <u>hatch</u>. A group of people watched from a window inside the hotel. They saw all the little ducklings come out of their shells.
>
> Mother Duck must really like the Ritz. It was the second year she made her nest there.

1. What do you think a <u>marsh</u> is? What context clues helped you know its meaning?

_____

_____

2. What do you think <u>down</u> means in this passage? What words help explain its meaning?

_____

_____

3. How can you use the sentence "They saw all the little ducklings come out of their shells" to figure out the meaning of <u>hatch</u>?

_____

_____

Guided Instruction 2

R3.LC   Learn new vocabulary and concepts indirectly by reading books and other print sources.

Introduction

You can use **context clues** to find the meaning of new words. Look at how the new word is used. Then think about the meaning of the words and sentences around it. Use these clues to find the meaning of the word.

As you saw on pages 55–57, graphic organizers help you use context clues.

- Write the new or unfamiliar word in the first box.
- Write context clues you find in the second box.
- Write what you think the word means in the third box.

Here's How

Read these sentences. What context clues can help you figure out the meaning of <u>inventor</u>?

Thomas Edison was an <u>inventor</u>. He was always thinking up new things to make. In the 1880s, Edison wanted to get electricity to people's homes for the first time. He worked hard to make that happen.

Think About It

Word	Context Clues	Meaning
<u>inventor</u>	He was always thinking up new things. He made it happen.	a person who thinks up and makes new things to use

Try This Strategy

Scan and Skim

When you **scan and skim,** you read quickly to get an idea of what an article is about and what you will learn.

- First scan the article. Look at the title and any pictures. These features will help you identify the topic.
- Next, skim the article. Look for key words about the topic. These key words will give you an idea of what you will learn about the topic.

Read the story. Use the Reading Guide for tips. The tips will help you scan and skim and use context clues as you read.

Reading Guide

When you look at the title and picture, what topic do you think you'll read about? Look for key words in the article to get an idea about the topic.

How does reading the whole paragraph help you understand the meaning of curious?

What does experiments mean? Can you find a word in the next sentence that means the same thing?

What made Thomas Edison a genius?

Thomas Edison's Mistake

Thomas Edison was an <u>inventor</u>. He was always thinking up new things to make. In the 1880s, Edison wanted to get electricity to people's homes for the first time. He worked hard to make that happen.

Edison didn't mind working hard. When he was only 12, he got his first job. It was on the Grand Trunk Railroad in Michigan. Each day, Edison <u>boarded</u> the train. Then he would sell newspapers and candy to passengers <u>bound</u> for Detroit.

Even as a boy, Thomas Edison had a <u>curious</u> nature. That meant he was always asking questions. He wanted to know everything. He was always searching for answers. Edison's curious nature got him into trouble on the train one day.

Edison had set up a lab in a baggage car to do <u>experiments</u>. One day, something went wrong with one of his tests. He <u>accidentally</u> set the train on fire. He didn't mean to do it. It was a good thing that no one got hurt.

Thomas Edison was a <u>genius</u>. He was smarter than most people. He used his brain to do great things during his life. But even smart people do dumb things sometimes.

Answer the questions on the next page.

Practice the Skill 2

R3.LC Learn new vocabulary and concepts indirectly by reading books and other print sources.

Practice using context clues by answering questions about the article you just read. Read each question. Circle the letter of the best answer.

1. From the clues in the story, you can tell that boarded most likely means —

A sold
B got on
C searched
D got into trouble

2. Which word in the sentence with bound gives the best clue to its meaning?

A *sell*
B *newspapers*
C *candy*
D *Detroit*

3. A curious person is someone who —

A wants to know all about things
B likes riding on trains
C starts fires
D causes trouble

4. Which word in the article means almost the same as experiments and is a clue to its meaning?

A *answers*
B *baggage*
C *tests*
D *things*

5. What is the best meaning of accidentally?

A On purpose
B By mistake
C In a silly way
D In time

6. On a separate sheet of paper, tell the meaning of genius. Tell how you used context clues to figure out the meaning.

Students sampled food at the Prince William County food show.

STUDENTS MAKE THEIR OWN MENU

PRINCE WILLIAM COUNTY, VA— These students can't complain about their cafeteria food. After all, they helped choose it! In Prince William County, Virginia, the 16th annual food show took place. Students, parents, and teachers tasted 30 different breakfast and lunch foods. The items they liked best will go on the county's school menus next year.

The favorites this year included pizza sticks, popcorn chicken, and banana and kiwi halves. "It's all pretty good," said seventh-grader Jeriko Mafnas. Jeriko was attending his fourth food show.

Serena Struthers is the Director of Food Services. She says that school officials use the show to see what <u>nutritious</u> foods children will eat. Many of the foods offered are healthier versions of foods students already eat. Food services officials try to pick foods that are healthy, cheap, and easy to make in school cafeterias.

Write About It

What is the meaning of <u>nutritious</u>? What clues in the paragraph helped you find the definition?

LADDERS to SUCCESS

LESSON
4
Using Context Clues

Show What You Learned

R3.LC   Learn new vocabulary and concepts indirectly by reading books and other print sources.

Read this story about a neighbor and the street she lives on. Then answer the questions on the next page.

IT HAPPENED ON SPRING STREET

Gale's dad was watching the news. "Come quick," he yelled. Gale and her sister Rita ran into the den.

"Look," her dad said, pointing to the TV. "It's Spring Street. There's Mrs. Russo at her window. They want her to leave her house, but she's being <u>stubborn</u>. She refuses to go."

Mrs. Russo had been at her first-floor window for as long as Gale could remember. She was at the window when Gale left for school in the morning. She was there when Gale returned in the afternoon. She sat there while the kids played in the street. She was still sitting there at night when Gale said goodbye to her friends and went inside.

When Gale was really little, she thought Mrs. Russo was <u>attached</u> to her chair with glue. Gale asked her mom if Mrs. Russo ever went to bed. Her mom said she went to bed after all the noisy kids went home and Spring Street was <u>hushed</u>.

Gale didn't live on Spring Street anymore. No one did, except for Mrs. Russo. The city was tearing down the buildings. The city was <u>destroying</u> the whole neighborhood.

Gale watched as a man in a black suit tried to talk to Mrs. Russo. She <u>ignored</u> him. She stared straight ahead and didn't answer. Then the camera moved to a TV <u>reporter</u>. He said the <u>wrecking ball</u> would be on Spring Street the next morning. It was going to start knocking buildings down.

"Maybe because of Mrs. Russo they won't tear down the buildings. Then we can move back," Gale said. Just then, the camera moved back to Mrs. Russo's window. Two police officers were standing behind her. She was shaking her head as they lifted her gently from her chair. Then she was gone. The window was empty, and the building was <u>vacant</u>.

Read each question. Circle the letter of the best answer.

1. Which words from the story help explain the meaning of <u>stubborn</u>?

   A *watching the news*

   B *ran into the den*

   C *pointing to the TV*

   D *refuses to go*

2. In this story, the best meaning for <u>attached</u> is —

   A holding

   B close

   C stuck

   D tied

3. Which words in the story mean almost the same as <u>destroying</u> and are a clue to its meaning?

   A *still sitting*

   B *went to*

   C *didn't live*

   D *tearing down*

4. From the clues in the story, you can tell that <u>ignored</u> means —

   A paid no attention to

   B stared at for a long time

   C talked to

   D lived near

5. Which word in the story is the opposite of <u>hushed</u> and helps you know its meaning?

   A *really*

   B *little*

   C *ever*

   D *noisy*

6. Which of these words from the story is *not* a context clue to the meaning of <u>reporter</u>?

   A *news*

   B *buildings*

   C *camera*

   D *TV*

7. A <u>wrecking ball</u> is —

   A something children play with in the street

   B something used to knock down buildings

   C a kind of television camera

   D someone who makes people move

8. On a separate sheet of paper, explain how you used context clues to figure out the meaning of <u>vacant</u>.

LADDERS to SUCCESS

LESSON
5
Identifying
Main Ideas and
Details

Show What You Know

R3.1   Identify main ideas and supporting details in informational texts.

Before you begin this lesson, take this quiz to show what you know about identifying main ideas and details. Read the story. Then answer the questions.

The New Baby-sitter

Mom and Dad were going out for dinner. A new baby-sitter was coming. I told Mom that I was too old for a baby-sitter. She said, "Nice try, Joe."

Baby-sitters can be strange. The last baby-sitter smelled funny. The one before that made us eat creamed spinach. It was gross. My little sister liked it, but she's weird. The one before the spinach lady didn't let us watch TV. She told Mom I was "quite a handful." I am NOT!

I wondered how bad this baby-sitter would be. I could stay in my room. I'd listen to music all night. I'd pretend I was the boss. Maybe she'd leave me alone.

I listened at my bedroom door as my parents left. I heard footsteps come down the hall. I held my breath and hoped she'd walk by. No such luck. I backed away as my door opened. I shut my eyes. I expected the worst.

Circle the letter of the best answer.

1. Which sentence best states the main idea of the story?

   A Joe doesn't want his parents to go out.

   B Joe wants the baby-sitter to leave.

   C Joe is not looking forward to having a baby-sitter.

   D Joe doesn't like to eat vegetables.

2. Which detail tells more about the main idea of the story?

   A *Mom and Dad were going out.*

   B *I wondered how bad this baby-sitter would be.*

   C *I backed away as my door opened.*

   D *The last baby-sitter smelled funny.*

3. The main idea of the second paragraph is —

   A baby-sitters can be strange

   B a new baby-sitter was coming

   C baby-sitters can smell funny

   D I can be "quite a handful"

4. What is the main idea of the last paragraph?

   A Joe was excited.

   B Joe was nervous.

   C Joe was lazy.

   D Joe was confident.

LADDERS to SUCCESS

LESSON

5
Identifying
Main Ideas and
Details

Guided Instruction 1

R3.1   Identify main ideas and supporting details in informational texts.

Introduction

A **main idea** is the most important idea in a passage or paragraph. A **detail** is an idea that tells about the main idea. You can **identify main ideas and details** by thinking about the "big idea" and finding "little ideas" that tell more about it.

To identify main ideas and details,

- Think about what the paragraph or passage is mostly about.
- Pay attention to the title, the first sentence, or the last sentence of a paragraph. Sometimes the main idea is stated here.
- To find details, try to answer questions about the main idea. Look for facts and examples that answer *who, what, when, where, why,* and *how*.

Here's How

Read this paragraph. What is the main idea? What details tell about it?

Sunny days were good luck for the team. Marty paused. He looked out the window at the end of the hall. He was glad to see it was a sunny day. Marty knew they needed all the luck they could get.

Think About It

1. The paragraph tells about sunny days and luck.

2. The first sentence tells that sunny days were good luck for the team. This is the main idea.

3. The details tell that Marty sees it's a sunny day and is glad.

Try This Strategy

Predict

When you **predict,** you make a guess about what you will read.

- Read the title so you know what the passage will be about.
- After each paragraph, predict what you will read in the next paragraph.

Read the story. Use the Reading Guide for tips. The tips will help you predict and identify main ideas and details as you read.

Reading Guide

Use the title and the picture to help you predict what this story will be about.

Marty does lots of special things on game day. The description of what he does has details that support the main idea.

Predict what Marty will probably do on the way to the game.

Think about what this story is mostly about. The main idea tells about Marty and game day.

Marty's Way On Game Day

Marty started his game-day **routine**. He always did everything the exact same way. He put on his uniform. He put on his lucky sock and lucky sneakers. Then he put on his lucky hat. He walked backward out of his room. Then he walked sideways down the hall.

Sunny days were good luck for the team. Marty paused. He looked out the window at the end of the hall. He was glad to see it was a sunny day. Marty knew they needed lots of luck.

Marty went into the kitchen. He crossed his fingers as he opened the refrigerator. He hoped there was some salami. Marty's game-day rules said he had to eat half a salami-and-cheese sandwich. Then, he had to share the other half with pigeons on his way to the ballpark. Whistling his lucky tune, Marty made his sandwich. Then he grabbed some grapes. These weren't for good luck. He just liked them.

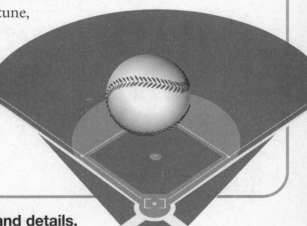

Now use what you learned to identify main ideas and details.

Answer the questions on the next page.

Practice the Skill 1

Practice identifying the main ideas and details of the story you just read.

EXAMPLE

What sentence in the first paragraph tells the main idea of the paragraph?

A Marty started his game-day routine.

B He put on his lucky sock and lucky sneakers.

C Then he put on his lucky hat.

D Then he walked sideways down the hall.

Review the paragraph to find out what it is mostly about.

It tells what Marty always *does* before a game.

Look for the main idea. The other ideas should tell about this idea.

The main idea is that Marty follows a routine on game day.

Find details that tell more about the main idea.

The *details describe* how he *gets dressed* and how he walks. They *tell* more about the main idea.

Now read each question. Circle the letter of the best answer.

1. Which detail tells more about the idea that Marty believes in luck?

A Marty paused.

B Marty looked out the window.

C Marty went into the kitchen.

D Marty crossed his fingers.

2. What is the main idea of the third paragraph?

A Marty's routine includes food.

B Marty likes grapes.

C Marty always eats his lunch on the way to the game.

D Marty thinks pigeons are lucky.

3. What is the main idea of the story?

A Marty's team needs lots of luck.

B Marty thinks his team will win if he follows his routine.

C Marty enjoys playing baseball on sunny days.

D Marty loves to eat sandwiches.

4. Which sentence from the story best supports the story's main idea?

A *He always did everything the exact same way.*

B *Marty knew they needed luck.*

C *He hoped there was some salami.*

D *Then he grabbed some grapes.*

PANCAKE PRIDE

Some people in Pancake Town, U.S.A., want their water tower to look like a stack of pancakes.

BURTON, OH—People flip for the pancakes in Burton, Ohio. In fact, many people call the town Pancake Town, U.S.A. That's why people there have a fun idea. They want to paint pancakes on their water tower.

The water tower would look like a stack of pancakes. The sides would drip with syrup.

Maple syrup season is a busy time in Burton. People come from miles around. The town serves tens of thousands of pancakes.

Now people could come for more than just pancakes. They could come to see the water tower. People who like the idea say it would make Burton a popular place. Not everyone likes the idea, though. Some call it bad taste.

Write About It

Now practice the skill. Use information from this news article. Fill in this graphic organizer. First, tell the main idea of the article. Then write three details that tell more about the main idea.

Main Idea:
Detail: The town serves tens of thousands of pancakes.
Detail:
Detail:

LADDERS to SUCCESS

LESSON

5
Identifying
Main Ideas and
Details

Ladder to Success

R3.1   Identify main ideas and supporting details in informational texts.

Review

Most things you read have a main idea and details. **Identifying the main ideas and details** can help you understand what you read. First try to find the main idea. As you continue to read, find facts and examples that tell more about it.

Review the steps you can use to identify main ideas and details.

- Read the passage or the paragraph. Decide what it is mostly about.
- Find the most important idea. You might find it in the title, in the first sentence, in the first paragraph, or in the last paragraph.
- Ask *who, what, when, where, why,* and *how*? about the main idea. These facts and examples are details that tell more about the main idea.

Practice 1

Read the passage. After you read, look at the first sentence to find the main idea. Then ask questions about the main idea to find supporting details.

> The Chesapeake Bay Bridge Tunnel is amazing. It's a bridge and a tunnel! It's the longest bridge in the world. In two spots, it dips below the water. Builders did this so large boats could get by. Putting the bridge under the water was smart. To do this, builders had to build islands. One island even has a gift shop!

Using the chart below, write the main idea in the top oval. Write the supporting details in the ovals below it.

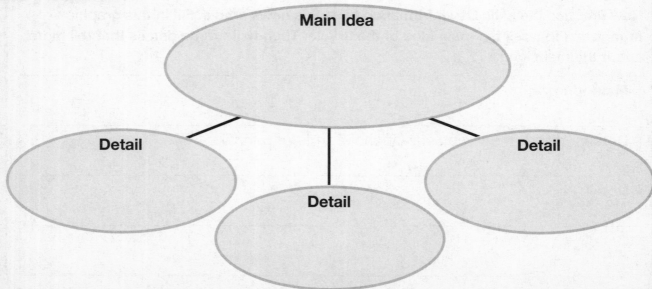

Main Idea

Detail

Detail

Detail

Practice 2

Read the story. What is the main idea? What details tell more about the main idea?

Lora was always inventing things. Her first invention was to help her mother. Her mother couldn't hold a shopping bag and an umbrella, and find her keys at the same time. Lora's special umbrella didn't need to be held. The handle sat on the user's shoulder. Lora wanted to call it the "UN–Brella."

Lora's next invention was for eating. She created a **utensil** with a spoon on one end and a fork on the other. It made eating soup and salad easier. As she ate, she simply flipped it over. She couldn't decide whether to call it the "Eat All" or the "Flipoon."

Fill in this graphic organizer to identify the main idea and details.

Main Idea

Detail	Detail	Detail

Practice 3

Read the passage. Then identify the main idea and details to answer the questions. Make a graphic organizer on a separate sheet of paper to organize your thoughts.

Life as an insect can be swell. Insects can fly and jump. Some can even walk on water. But life as an insect can also be tough. One minute you're munching on a tasty leaf. The next minute, you're some bird's lunch! Staying safe is important. Insects have many ways to do this.

Some insects give off a smelly chemical when an animal or other insect tries to eat them. Others fight back, with fangs, teeth, or pincers. Some insects are poisonous. Most animals won't snack on them! Other clever insects **imitate** poisonous insects. They trick animals into being afraid to eat them.

Some insects stay safe by hiding in plain sight. For example, one insect sits on a plant stem and blends right in. It looks just like the leaves around it! Another is great at blending into the background. This insect looks just like a stick! Even scientists who study insects sometimes have trouble finding it when it hides.

1. What is the main idea of the passage?

_____

_____

2. What is the main idea of the last paragraph?

_____

_____

3. What are two details in the last paragraph?

_____

_____

LADDERS to SUCCESS

LESSON

5

Identifying
Main Ideas and
Details

Guided Instruction 2

R3.1   Identify main ideas and supporting details in informational texts.

Introduction

When you read, you will find **main ideas and details**. The **main idea** is the most important idea. **Details** tell more about the main idea.

As you saw on pages 69–71, graphic organizers help you identify main ideas and details.

- Review what you've read. Decide what it is mostly about.
- Find the main idea and write it in the top circle. The main idea might be found in the title, the first sentence, the first paragraph, or the last paragraph. It is the most important idea.
- Look for facts and examples that tell more about the main idea. Write these details in the bottom circles.

Here's How

Read this paragraph. What are two details that support the main idea?

Plants must have sunlight. Sunlight gives the plant energy. The plant uses energy from the sun to make food. The food a plant makes is sugar.

Think About It

Main Idea
Plants must have sunlight.

Detail	Detail
Sunlight gives the plant energy.	The plant uses the energy for food.

Try This Strategy

Monitor and Clarify

When you **monitor and clarify,** you make sure you understand the most important ideas and the details in something you read.

- Tell the main ideas of each paragraph in your own words.
- Reread any section that you did not understand.

Read the story. Use the Reading Guide for tips. The tips will help you monitor and clarify and identify main ideas and details as you read.

Reading Guide

Look for the main idea at the beginning of the article.

Did you understand why plants need nutrients?

How does the stem help the plants get what they need?

Think about what you have read. Restate the main idea of the passage.

What All Plants Need

All plants have the same basic needs. They need water, **nutrients,** sunlight, and air.

Plants get water in two ways. They absorb it through their leaves. They also take water in through their roots.

The roots take in nutrients. Most plants find their nutrients in soil. Plants use nutrients to grow, make seeds, and produce fruit.

The water and nutrients taken in by the roots are sent to different parts of the plant. They travel through a system of tubes, like the water pipes in your house. The most important "pipe" in most plants is the stem.

Sometimes you eat a plant's stem, like celery. Sometimes you may not realize that a plant has a stem. For example, did you know that a tree's trunk is its stem?

Plants must have sunlight. Sunlight gives plants energy. The plant uses energy from the sun to make food. The food a plant makes is sugar.

Plants can't survive without air. The chemicals in the air help plants grow and make food. Plants get most of their air by absorbing it through their leaves. They can also absorb air through their roots.

Answer the questions on the next page.

LADDERS
to SUCCESS

LESSON

5
Identifying
Main Ideas and
Details

R3.1   Identify main ideas and supporting details in informational texts.

Practice the Skill 2

Practice identifying main ideas and details by answering questions about the article you just read. Read each question. Circle the letter of the best answer.

1. Choose the main idea that this detail supports: *The chemicals in the air help plants grow and make food*.

   A Plants must have sunlight.

   B The roots also take in nutrients.

   C Plants can't survive without air.

   D Plants get water in two main ways.

2. Which detail best supports the main idea that the most important part of most plants is the stem?

   A Water and nutrients travel through the stem.

   B Sometimes you eat a plant's stem.

   C A tree's trunk is its stem.

   D You may not realize that a plant has a stem.

3. The main ideas in paragraphs 2, 3, and 4 are placed —

   A at the end of the passage

   B at the end of the paragraph

   C at the beginning of the paragraph

   D in the middle of the paragraph

4. What is the main idea of the whole article?

   A All plants have stems.

   B All plants need sunlight.

   C Plants can't live without air.

   D All plants have the same basic needs.

5. One clue to the main idea of the whole article is in —

   A the third paragraph

   B the title

   C the last sentence

   D the second paragraph

6. On a separate sheet of paper, make a web. Draw a large center circle. Draw six smaller circles around it. In the large center circle, write about the main idea of the article. In the smaller circles, write about the main idea of each paragraph, starting with Paragraph 2.

A new museum displays action figures of all kinds.

ACTION FIGURE Museum Opens

PAULS VALLEY, OK—The world's first action figure museum opened recently. It is in the small town of Pauls Valley, Oklahoma. The Toy and Action Figure Museum holds more than 7,000 action figures. It has more toys than the entire population of Pauls Valley.

The idea for the museum came in 2000. Toy collector Kevin Stark wanted to display all his action figures. Pauls Valley residents wanted a tourist attraction for their town. The town worked with Stark to build the museum in an old department store.

The museum has colorful **murals** on the walls. There are rooms for popular action figures. There is also an Action Figure Hall of Fame. One room is filled with blocks. Visitors can build their own superheroes and display them on the shelves.

In this museum, playing with the display items is allowed! The museum accepts toy donations to replace action figures that break or disappear.

Write About It

Write a sentence that identifies the main idea of the article. Then, write two sentences that give details about the main idea.

LADDERS to SUCCESS

LESSON 5
Identifying Main Ideas and Details

Show What You Learned

R3.1   Identify main ideas and supporting details in informational texts.

Read this article about magnets. Then answer the questions on the next page.

The Power of Magnets

Magnets are pieces of metal with special powers. Magnets attract other types of metal. Iron, nickel, and steel are strongly attracted by magnets. Some rocks and minerals have these metals in them. So magnets also attract them. Some other rocks and minerals that magnets attract are hematite, magnetite, and pyrite.

Magnets come in three shapes. Bar magnets are shaped like rods. Horseshoe magnets are shaped like the letter "U." Ring magnets are shaped like flat donuts. All magnets have two ends. These ends are called poles. They are North and South. On a bar or horseshoe magnet, the poles are the two ends. On a ring magnet, the poles are the front and back faces.

Two North poles push each other away. Two South poles will push each other away. A North and a South pole will attract each other.

Earth is a magnet. Earth's poles are like the poles on a magnet. The South of a magnet will always point toward Earth's magnetic North pole. That's how a compass works.

Magnets that you buy in the store are **permanent** magnets. They stay magnetic for a long time. A **temporary** magnet stays magnetic for a short time. You can make a temporary magnet if you have a permanent magnet and something that is drawn to a magnet, like an iron nail. Rub the magnet along the nail, in the same direction, for fifty strokes. The nail will stay magnetic for a little while.

Some magnets are made of a special material that makes them very strong. One kind of magnet is so strong that if it is held next to a computer, it can erase the computer's memory.

Read each question. Circle the letter of the best answer.

1. The title suggests that this article is about —

   A super powers
   B magnets
   C people and magnets
   D staying strong

2. What is the first paragraph mostly about?

   A Rocks and minerals
   B What magnets attract
   C Different kinds of metal
   D What rocks attract

3. The main idea of the second paragraph is stated in the —

   A first sentence
   B second sentence
   C fifth sentence
   D last sentence

4. Which detail supports the idea that the Earth is a magnet?

   A *Iron, nickel, and steel are strongly attracted by magnets.*
   B *All magnets have two ends.*
   C *Two South poles will push each other away.*
   D *That's how a compass works.*

5. The details in the fifth paragraph support the main idea that —

   A you can buy a magnet in a store
   B it's fun to make temporary magnets at home
   C magnets can be temporary or permanent
   D permanent magnets are better than temporary magnets

6. Which detail supports the main idea of the second paragraph?

   A *Bar magnets are shaped like rods.*
   B *All magnets have two ends.*
   C *They are North and South.*
   D *These ends are called poles.*

7. Which statement best tells a main idea of the article?

   A Magnets are important to us.
   B Most people enjoy using magnets.
   C Magnets are used in a compass.
   D Never hold a magnet near a computer.

8. On a separate sheet of paper, tell the main idea of the article in your own words. Give at least three details from the article to support the main idea.

Show What You Know

R3.2   Make predictions, draw conclusions, and make inferences about events and characters.

Before you begin this lesson, take this quiz to show what you know about drawing conclusions. Read this story about a surprise visitor. Then answer the questions.

THE VISITOR

Alan stood at the window. He peered at the small animal at the edge of the trees. He had no idea what it was. He knew it wasn't any of the usual critters. It was bigger than a squirrel or chipmunk. It was not a cat. It did look a little like a dog.

"Dad!" Alan whispered.

The animal's ears perked up. It turned toward the window. Alan didn't move a muscle.

Just then, Alan's dad popped into the living room. "Did you call me?" he shouted. Alan's shoulders sagged as the tiny animal darted off into the trees. "Sorry," his dad said.

Alan described the animal as best he could. "It was light brown," he said. "It had a pointed snout and small pointed ears. Oh, and it had a small bushy tail."

"I'm guessing it was a baby fox," his dad said. "Want to come to the mall?" his dad asked.

"Nah," Alan said. "I think I'll just hang around here and see what happens."

Circle the letter of the best answer.

1. Why didn't Alan know that the animal was a baby fox?

   A It was hiding behind a tree.

   B Alan had probably never seen a baby fox.

   C Alan was too far away.

   D It darted away before Alan got a good look at it.

2. From the clues in the story, you can figure out that —

   A foxes and dogs are in the same family

   B baby foxes cannot hear well

   C Dad doesn't believe Alan's story

   D Dad has never seen a fox

3. Why does Alan whisper, "Dad"?

   A Dad is asleep.

   B Alan's not supposed to yell in the house.

   C He doesn't want to scare away the fox.

   D He's afraid of the fox.

4. Why doesn't Alan want to go to the mall with his dad?

   A Because he has other plans

   B Because he doesn't like shopping

   C Because he hopes to see the fox again

   D Because he is feeling lazy

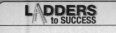

LESSON

6

Drawing Conclusions

Guided Instruction 1

R3.2   Make predictions, draw conclusions, and make inferences about events and characters.

A **conclusion** is something the writer wants you to know or understand, but does not tell you. When you **draw a conclusion,** you figure something out, without the writer telling you.

To draw a conclusion,

- Think about what you read.
- Think about what you already know about the story or topic.
- Combine what you read with what you already know to come up with new ideas. These ideas are conclusions.

Here's How

Read these sentences. Draw a conclusion about Abraham Lincoln's name.

You probably know many stories about Abraham Lincoln. Here's a story you may not have heard about Abe Lincoln, the boy.

Think About It

1. I read that Abraham Lincoln is sometimes called Abe.

2. I know that children often have nicknames that are short for their full name.

3. I can draw the conclusion that Abe is a nickname for Abraham. I can also conclude that Abraham Lincoln was called Abe as a boy.

Use Prior Knowledge

When you **use prior knowledge,** you use what you know to understand what you read.

- Think of what you already know about the topic.
- Think about things that a story or topic reminds you of.
- Combine information you read and what you know to arrive at new ideas and draw a conclusion.

Read the story. Use the Reading Guide for tips. The tips will help you use prior knowledge and draw conclusions as you read.

 Reading Guide

NOT SO SERIOUS ABE

You probably know many stories about Abraham Lincoln. Here's a story you may not have heard about Abe Lincoln, the boy.

Abe was getting taller. He grew so tall that his head bumped the ceiling. His stepmother Sarah said, "Watch out, Abe. Your head will leave marks. I can't reach up to clean them!"

Think about why Sarah tells Abe to watch out. Then think about what you know about houses today.

Later, Abe's stepbrother Johnny came home with his feet covered in mud. Abe got an idea.

"Want to walk on the ceiling?" Abe asked Johnny.

"I can't do that!" said Johnny. "My feet are muddy."

Look for details that tell what Abe wants Johnny to do. Think about people you know who do things like this.

"Exactly," Abe said, with a twinkle in his eye. Then he picked Johnny up and flipped him over. Johnny's feet touched the ceiling. "Now take a few steps."

Think about what happens when someone walks on something with muddy feet.

Abe and Johnny didn't tell anyone what they'd done until dinner. When the family sat down to eat, the boys couldn't keep their joke a secret.

Notice how Sarah felt about what Abe did. Think about what this tells about her.

At first, Sarah was angry. Soon, she was laughing, too. Abe promised to repaint the ceiling the next day.

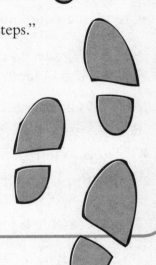

Now use what you learned to draw conclusions.

Answer the questions on the next page.

Practice the Skill 1

R3.2   Make predictions, draw conclusions, and make inferences about events and characters.

Practice drawing conclusions about the passage you just read.

EXAMPLE

From what you read in the passage, what conclusion can you draw about the house Abe Lincoln lived in when he was a boy?

A It had only one room.

B It had low ceilings.

C It had mud floors.

D It had dark-colored ceilings.

Think about the important ideas in the passage. Think about the details.

The details say that Abe's head bumped the ceiling.

Think about what you already know about this idea.

I know that even really tall people don't bump their heads in most houses today.

Combine what you know with what you read. Come up with a new idea, or a conclusion.

I can draw the conclusion that the ceilings in his house were probably low.

Now read each question. Circle the letter of the best answer.

1. You can draw the conclusion that young Abe Lincoln —

A was very serious

B was not close to his family

C liked to play jokes

D did not like getting dirty

2. What probably happens when Johnny does what Abe tells him to do?

A He leaves muddy footprints on the ceiling.

B He gets a bad headache.

C His feet get dirty.

D He walks backwards.

3. What can you tell about Johnny from the details in the story?

A He's a troublemaker.

B He's smaller than Abe.

C He has big feet.

D He is always covered in mud.

4. What probably happens during dinner?

A Mud falls on the dinner table.

B The boys tell each other a secret.

C Sarah scolds the boys for making the floors muddy.

D The boys tell Sarah what they did.

A coyote wandered through Central Park.

A Coyote Visits Central Park

NEW YORK, NY—A wild coyote was found in a strange place recently. At first, people thought it was a dog. Coyotes look a lot like big dogs. But they are actually wild animals. They can be very dangerous.

Residents near Central Park in New York City saw the coyote first. Police tracked it for more than an hour before they caught it. Then they brought it to the Queens Zoo.

No one knows how the coyote reached the city. Some think he crossed a bridge over the Hudson River. Others think he might have swum.

No matter how he arrived, the coyote was looking for food when he got there. Coyotes eat almost everything. They eat trash, mice, and rats. Lately, coyotes have been showing up in many cities.

Write About It

Now practice the skill. Use information from this news article. Complete this graphic organizer. Write what you read and what you know that can help you draw a conclusion.

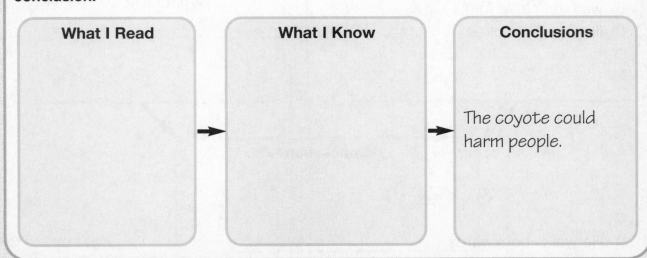

What I Read	What I Know	Conclusions
		The coyote could harm people.

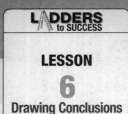
LESSON
6
Drawing Conclusions

Ladder to Success

R3.2   Make predictions, draw conclusions, and make inferences about events and characters.

Review

A writer doesn't always tell you everything. Sometimes you have to come up with ideas on your own. You combine the information the author gives you with things you already know. Then you come up with new ideas. This is called **drawing conclusions.**

Review the steps you can use to draw conclusions.

- Think about the ideas and details in a story or article.
- Think about what you already know about the topic.
- Put together what you read and what you know to draw a conclusion.

Practice 1

Read the following passage. Look for details about state flowers and state trees. Think about what you already know about state flowers and trees. Draw a conclusion about how states chose their state flowers and trees.

> What do Maine, Mississippi, and Virginia have in common? They are the only states that chose one plant to be both their state flower and their state tree. Maine chose the eastern white pine. Mississippi chose the magnolia. Virginia chose the American dogwood. Virginia officials hoped their choice would make Virginians proud. They also hoped other Americans would want to learn more about their state.

Fill in the graphic organizer below. Write details from the passage. Write what you already know. Then make a good guess about how the states chose their flowers and trees.

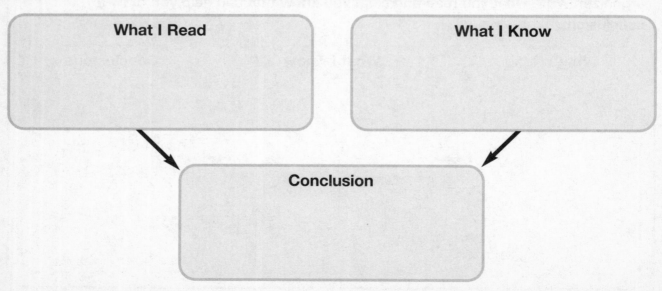

What I Read

What I Know

Conclusion

Practice 2

Read the passage. What conclusions can you draw about where the narrator lives and one of her bad habits?

Of all the trees in town, only one is perfect. I don't like pine trees. They drop their needles everywhere. Maple trees are nice, but kind of plain. Oak trees are too big. I like the birch. It has a slender white trunk that is smeared with black splotches and streaks. Sometimes, these marks look like faces. The perfect tree in town is the birch in front of the library. It looks like Mr. Alf, the librarian. Maybe he is reminding me not to be late returning my library books *again!*

Fill in this graphic organizer to draw a conclusion about the narrator.

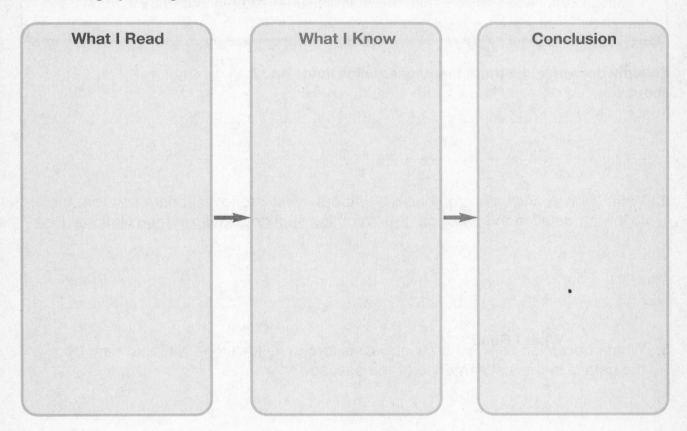

What I Read	What I Know	Conclusion

Practice 3

Read the passage. Then draw conclusions to answer the questions. Make a graphic organizer on a separate sheet of paper to organize your thoughts.

A geyser is a spot where a hot spring bursts out from the ground and sprays straight up into the air. This feature was named in Iceland. The word *geyser* is an Icelandic word that means "to gush." There are two other spots in the world that have geyser fields. One is in New Zealand. The other is in the Wyoming section of Yellowstone National Park.

There are about 1,000 geysers in the world. Almost 500 of them are in Yellowstone. One of the best-known geysers in Yellowstone is Old Faithful.

Old Faithful is big. It can shoot as high as 180 feet in the air. And the eruption can contain up to 8,700 gallons of water. But many geysers have larger eruptions than that. Old Faithful isn't popular because it's the largest. People like Old Faithful because it erupts more often than any other big geyser in the area.

1. How do you know there are geyser fields in Iceland?

_____

_____

2. What is one conclusion you can draw about Yellowstone National Park from the following detail in the passage: the Wyoming section of Yellowstone National Park?

_____

_____

3. What conclusion can you draw about visitors to Yellowstone National Park from the details in the last sentence of the passage?

_____

_____

Guided Instruction 2

R3.2   Make predictions, draw conclusions, and make inferences about events and characters.

Sometimes when you read, you can find out things that are not written on the page. You can **draw conclusions** to fill in missing details. You do this by combining what you read with ideas you already know.

As you saw on pages 83–85, graphic organizers help you draw conclusions.

- First write details you read.
- Then write information you already know about the idea.
- Put these together to draw a conclusion. Write your conclusion.

Here's How

Read these sentences. What is one conclusion you can draw about Beth?

Beth knew something was wrong with Pele. She'd been watching her carefully for weeks.

Think About It

What I Read	**What I Know**	**Conclusions**
Beth knew something was wrong with Pele. She'd been watching her carefully for weeks.	People who care about their pets watch them carefully and worry about them.	Beth takes good care of her guppies. Beth cares about her fish.

Monitor and Clarify

When you **monitor and clarify,** you make sure you understand the most important ideas and the details in a story.

- Ask yourself whether you understand the ideas in each paragraph.
- Try retelling the main ideas in your own words to make sure you understand them.
- Reread any section you did not understand.

Read the story. Use the Reading Guide for tips that can help you monitor and clarify and draw conclusions as you read.

Reading Guide

Pele's Surprise

Did you understand why Beth named her favorite fish Pele? Would it help to reread this section?

Of all the guppies, Pele had always been Beth's favorite. She'd noticed her right away because she stood out. The other 8 guppies were all yellowish-orange, but Pele was yellowish-green. Beth had been reading about Hawaiian mythology. She named the fish after the goddess of fire, lightning, and volcanoes.

Beth knew something was wrong with Pele. She'd been watching her carefully for weeks. All the other guppies looked fine, the same as always. Beth was sure, though, that Pele was injured or sick. She dragged her mother to the fish tank.

"See, Mom?" she pointed. "Pele has funny little bumps, or something, near her tail. I think she's sick."

What makes Mom chuckle when she looks at Pele and the other fish?

Beth's Mom leaned close to the glass and looked carefully at Pele. She looked at some of the other guppies, then back at Pele. She started to chuckle. "Beth," She said. "I don't think Pele is sick at all."

"Well, then, what's wrong with my fish?" Beth asked, worried.

"What's 'wrong' is that she isn't a fish at all. She's a frog! At least she will be." Mom explained to Beth. "I think Pele's a tadpole! We better get her out of that tank."

Can you retell all the important parts of this story in your own words?

Answer the questions on the next page.

Practice the Skill 2

R3.2   Make predictions, draw conclusions, and make inferences about events and characters.

Practice drawing conclusions by answering questions about the story you just read. Read each question. Circle the letter of the best answer.

1. From the details in the first paragraph, you can draw the conclusion that —

   A Pele is Beth's only friend

   B Pele has been acting differently lately

   C Pele has tried to get out of the tank

   D Pele is not getting along with the other fish

2. Beth probably liked Pele best because —

   A Pele looked like a goddess

   B Pele looked different

   C Pele was a frog

   D Pele was named after a goddess

3. From details in the story, you can tell that Beth probably —

   A knows everything about fish

   B has been to Hawaii

   C likes reading mythology

   D has never had a pet before

4. Why does Beth's mom chuckle when she looks in the tank?

   A She thinks Pele looks funny with bumps.

   B She doesn't care about Beth's feelings.

   C She realizes Pele is not a guppy.

   D She thinks tadpoles are funny.

5. From the details in the story, you can tell that —

   A Pele has probably started to change

   B Pele is sick

   C Pele was injured a long time ago

   D the tadpoles are trying to hurt Pele

6. On a separate sheet of paper, tell why you think Beth didn't notice that Pele was a tadpole sooner.

Light bulbs today have a much shorter lifespan.

LIGHT BULB BURNS FOR 100 YEARS

FORT WORTH, TX—Fort Worth residents will be celebrating a special birthday. Its famous light bulb is turning 100! The **mysterious** bulb has been shining nonstop since September 21, 1908. It shows no signs of burning out.

The Texas light has had a long and interesting history. It was first switched on at an opera house nearly 100 years ago. The opera house later became a movie house. Many top actors stopped to admire the bulb's glow.

The movie house is now a museum. The bulb still works. "We have no idea why it has lasted so long," said Sarah Biles, who runs the museum. "That is the wonderful mystery of it."

The century-old bulb has not been burning the longest, however. The Livermore Centennial Bulb in California has been on since 1901. Second place doesn't seem to bother Texas residents, though. "Our bulb has a unique past and can hold its own, even if it is number two," Biles said.

Write About It

Read this sentence from the article: *The mysterious bulb has been shining nonstop since September 21, 1908.* The writer describes the bulb as mysterious. On a separate sheet of paper, explain how you think the writer drew this conclusion. Include things you already know about light bulbs as well as details from the article.

LADDERS to SUCCESS

Show What You Learned

LESSON
6
Drawing Conclusions

R3.2   Make predictions, draw conclusions, and make inferences about events and characters.

Read this story about a boy who tells a story. Then answer the questions on the next page.

Chris Tells a Tale

Dinners were never quiet at my house, especially on school nights. I always had to tell my parents about my day. I told them everything I learned in school. I told them everything I saw, heard, said, or did all day.

My brother Chris never talked. He just ate his dinner and listened. At the start of every dinner, Mom would ask him how his day was. "Fine," he'd say. Then she'd ask him if anything interesting had happened. "Nope!" or "Nothing!" was what he always said.

Then one night, Mom asked Chris how his day was. "Good!" he responded. Mom and I looked at each other. Mom asked if anything interesting or exciting had happened at school. "Yup," he replied. Dad put his fork down. My mouth dropped open. Mom looked like she was going to dance around the dinner table, which would have been something to see since her leg was still in a cast.

"A helicopter landed in our playground!" Chris began. "We all got to take rides. The pilot took us over the whole town, and I could see our house! Pretty cool." It was more than I'd ever heard Chris say at once, at least about something other than dumb football or baseball!

But Mom and Dad didn't look so happy any more. Mom had that same look she got when I was six and tried to hide oatmeal cookies in her computer's CD drive.

I could tell they were getting angrier by the minute. "The school should never have let you go for a helicopter ride without our **permission,**" Mom said. I was wondering about that when Chris started to laugh. Dad started to laugh, too. Then I did. Mom was the last to figure out that Chris had made the whole thing up!

Read each question. Circle the letter of the best answer.

1. What conclusion can you draw about the narrator from details in the first paragraph?

   A She is a good listener.

   B She is an A student.

   C She likes talking about herself.

   D She is usually quiet.

2. Which of these statements is probably true about the narrator and her brother?

   A They both like football.

   B They are both big talkers.

   C They both like playing jokes on their parents.

   D They are opposites when it comes to talking.

3. How do you know that Dad is surprised by Chris's response to Mom's questions?

   A He starts to dance.

   B He puts his fork down.

   C His mouth drops open.

   D He doesn't move.

4. Which of these is probably true about Mom?

   A She isn't easily excited.

   B She is taking dancing lessons.

   C She recently broke her leg.

   D She's a great cook.

5. From the details in the story, you can tell that Chris probably —

   A is a good dancer

   B likes sports

   C hopes to be a helicopter pilot

   D loves oatmeal cookies

6. Which of these is a clue you could use to conclude that Chris's story wasn't true before you got to the end?

   A The title

   B The first sentence

   C The second paragraph

   D The fifth paragraph

7. Why did Chris probably tell the helicopter story?

   A He thought it was true.

   B He didn't like dinner that night.

   C He thought it would be funny.

   D He wanted to be a helicopter pilot.

8. On a separate sheet of paper, write a conclusion about why Chris's parents are upset at first by his story. Use details from the story to support your conclusion.

Show What You Know

R3.2   Use knowledge of story structure, story elements, and key vocabulary to interpret stories.

Before you begin this lesson, take this quiz to show what you know about interpreting figurative language. Read this story about three pigs. Then answer the questions.

The Three Little Pigs: THE REAL STORY

Have you ever stopped to think about the three little pigs?

For one thing, the first two pigs weren't exactly as dumb as rocks. Think about it. Who did all the work?

The first little pig built a straw house. Straw is about as light as a feather. With a little mud here and a little mud there, he was done. He hardly broke a sweat.

The second little pig built his house with twigs. He just wove a pile of twigs together. Then he plunked a roof on top. He had his feet up and was sipping lemonade in no time.

The third little pig built his house out of bricks. Bricks are heavy and take a long time to stack. He spent days building a house that was as sturdy as a fort.

What happened next? The wolf came and blew down the straw hut and the twig cabin. The little pigs ran to their brother's brick house and were saved. Not a bad ending for two lazy pigs!

Circle the letter of the best answer.

1. If the two pigs were as *dumb as rocks* that would mean they —

   A had pointy heads

   B were not too smart

   C couldn't hammer a nail

   D were very quiet

2. The writer compares straw to a feather to show that —

   A straws and feathers come from the same place

   B straw isn't good for building

   C the first little pig didn't lift anything heavy

   D straw is cheap

3. In the story, what does the phrase *He hardly broke a sweat* mean?

   A He didn't work very hard.

   B He didn't need a shower.

   C He didn't break any pieces off.

   D He worked very hard.

4. A house *as sturdy as a fort* is —

   A strong and well built

   B very large

   C about to fall down

   D ugly

Guided Instruction 1

R3.2   Use knowledge of story structure, story elements, and key vocabulary to interpret stories.

Writers use **figurative language** to describe things in an interesting way. They use colorful words that create a picture in your mind. When you **interpret figurative language,** you figure out what these words mean.

To interpret figurative language,

- Look for words that are used in an unusual way.
- Look for words that compare two things. Think about how these things are alike. Make a picture in your mind from these words.
- In your own words, tell what you think the writer means.

Here's How

Read this passage. What two things does the writer compare to show you how Sandy feels?

"What was that?" Sandy yelled as she crouched down in the basket. Her brown eyes were as big as dinner plates.

Think About It

1. The writer compares Sandy's eyes to dinner plates.

2. Dinner plates are round and large. I picture Sandy with her eyes opened very wide, or round and large.

3. I know people open their eyes wide when they're scared or surprised. Sandy was probably scared or surprised by something.

Visualize

When you **visualize,** you picture in your mind what you are reading.

- Carefully read the writer's description. Think about the details.
- Use these details to form pictures in your mind.

Read the story. Use the Reading Guide for tips. The tips will help you visualize and interpret figurative language as you read.

Reading Guide

Look for words that describe the wind. Picture the wind giving a gentle kiss. Think about how a gentle kiss feels.

Picture what a scared rabbit might look like.

Look for words that tell you the writer is comparing smiles to something else.

UP, UP, AND AWAY!

One minute all she could hear was the soft wind as it blew gentle kisses on her cheeks. The next minute she heard a whoosh and a roar, like the sound of an angry lion about to charge.

"What was that?" Sandy yelled as she crouched down in the basket. Her brown eyes were as big as dinner plates.

"It's just the burner flame sending a boost of hot air to the top of the balloon," the pilot said. "We're rising higher now."

"You look like a scared rabbit," her brother Alex said. "Get up. This is way too cool to miss. Besides, didn't you say this was your dream?"

Sandy looked up at her parents. Their smiles were as wide as the valley below them. Then Sandy stood up. She didn't want to let her fears stop her form enjoying the ride.

Now use what you learned to interpret figurative language.

Answer the questions on the next page.

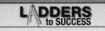

LESSON

7

Interpreting
Figurative Language

Practice the Skill 1

R3.2   Use knowledge of story structure, story elements, and key vocabulary to interpret stories.

Practice interpreting figurative language in the story you just read.

EXAMPLE

The writer compares the sound Sandy heard to an angry lion to let you know the sound was —

A soft and gentle

B weak

C strange

D loud and scary

Find words that make a picture in your mind.

I picture an angry lion roaring.

What idea does this picture help you understand? How does it make you feel?

This picture makes me understand how loud the sound was. It makes me feel afraid.

Use your own words to tell what the writer means.

The writer wants me to understand that the sound Sandy heard was loud and scary.

Now read each question. Circle the letter of the best answer.

1. Why does the writer say the wind *blew gentle kisses* on Sandy's cheeks?

    A To show that there was hardly any wind

    B To show that the wind was strong

    C To show that Sandy was hiding

    D To show that a storm was coming

2. The writer uses the image of a scared rabbit to help you understand —

    A how funny Sandy's brother is

    B how scary balloon rides are

    C how frightened Sandy looked

    D how small Sandy looked

3. Which words from the story mean "special and wonderful"?

    A *about to charge*

    B *to the top*

    C *a boost of hot air*

    D *way too cool*

4. In the story, the writer compares smiles to —

    A a flame

    B a balloon ride

    C a wide valley

    D a big basket

Turkeys HIT THE ROAD

Two dozen turkeys stopped traffic on the New Jersey Turnpike.

NEWARK, NJ—A traffic jam on the New Jersey Turnpike usually isn't news. This traffic jam was different, though. It happened right before Thanksgiving. The cause was turkeys.

Two dozen turkeys fell off a truck near Newark Airport. The turkeys were in crates. They did not die in the fall, but they stopped traffic dead.

Did the turkeys know that Thanksgiving was coming? If they did, maybe the fall was like a prison break for the turkeys. More likely, the turkeys just weren't packed safely onto the truck.

A tollbooth worker saw the turkeys in the road. Other workers got the turkeys off the road. Now the birds have to be returned to their owner. So far, the truck driver has not been found.

Write About It

Now practice the skill. Use information from this news article. Complete this graphic organizer. Fill in the meaning of figurative language from the article.

Figurative Language	Meaning
Maybe the fall was like a prison break for the turkeys.	

Ladder to Success

R3.2   Use knowledge of story structure, story elements, and key vocabulary to interpret stories.

Review

Figurative language is a fancy, descriptive way a writer expresses an idea.
Interpreting figurative language will help you understand a writer's ideas more fully.

Review the steps you can use to interpret figurative language.

- Look for words that are used in a funny or strange way.
- Look for words that compare one thing to another.
- Let the words paint pictures in your mind. Use the pictures to figure out what the writer wants you to know or feel.
- Explain what the writer means. Use your own words.

Practice 1

Read the following passage. As you read, look for figurative language that helps you picture the characters and setting. Think about what the pictures mean.

> The sun peeked over the horizon like a shy friend. "Come up! Come up!" the robins chirped.
>
> "What's wrong with you, sun?" the owl hooted. "I've been up all night and I'm tired. But I can't go to sleep until you come up."
>
> "That sun better show his face soon," the morning glory said. "If he doesn't, I think I'll burst. He knows I can't open up until he rises."

Use the chart below to tell what the figurative language from the passage means.

Figurative Language	Meaning
The sun peeked over the horizon like a shy friend.	
I think I'll burst.	

Practice 2

Read the passage. Look for figurative language that compares insects to other things.

Some insects sting. Their bites hurt and can even be dangerous. Some insects are just pests. They are like little flying motors that buzz near your ear. They may drive you crazy, but they don't hurt you.

Dragonflies are not dangerous. They're not pests either. They zip around the garden like tiny toy airplanes. Their see-through wings don't look strong enough to keep them up, but they do.

Dragonflies come in all colors. Some are black. Others are brown. Some dragonflies are ruby red, emerald green, or deep blue. Their bodies sparkle and **shimmer** like gems in the sunlight.

Use this graphic organizer to interpret figurative language.

Figurative Language	Things Compared	Meaning
They are like little flying motors that buzz your ear.		
They zip around the garden like tiny toy airplanes.		
Their bodies sparkle and shimmer like gems in sunlight.		

Practice 3

Read the poem. Then interpret figurative language to answer the questions. Make a graphic organizer on a separate sheet of paper to organize your thoughts.

Street Corners
What is it about street corners?
They attract kids like a magnet
attracts paper clips.

Maybe it's because
street corners are
like the **crow's nest**
at the top of a ship,
where pirates climbed
to look out at the sea
and watch for ships
that they could pounce on
like cats on a mouse.

Maybe it's because
street corners are
like lookout towers
above the castle walls,
where loyal knights stood
to keep watch
and protect the
the king and queen
from harm.

Or maybe it's because
street corners are the place
where all the other kids are.

1. What does it mean when the speaker says street corners *attract kids like a magnet attracts paper clips*?

_____

_____

2. What does the speaker compare pirates to in the poem? What does this help you understand?

_____

_____

3. Explain one of the underlined examples of figurative language in your own words.

_____

_____

Guided Instruction 2

R3.2   Use knowledge of story structure, story elements, and key vocabulary to interpret stories.

When writers use **figurative language,** they use words in an imaginative way. Figurative language helps you picture their ideas. When you read figurative language, think about the pictures and feelings the words bring to mind.

As you saw on pages 97–99, graphic organizers can help you interpret figurative language.

- Look for figurative language. Write it in the first box.
- In the second box, tell how the two things being compared are alike.
- In the last box, write the meaning of the figurative language in your own words.

Read these sentences. How does the idea of a friend help describe the beach?

Kerry loved the beach. The beach was her friend. She felt so comfortable here. She loved to feel the wet sand squishing through her toes. She loved the smell of the air.

Think About It

Figurative Language	How They Are Alike	Actual Meaning
The beach was her friend.	they make her feel happy they comfort her	Kerry felt happy and at home at the beach, as if she was with a friend.

Summarize

When you **summarize,** you retell what happens in a story or article, but with fewer words.

- As you read, look for the most important ideas and events.
- Tell what happens in the beginning, middle, and end of what you read.
- Use your own words. Leave out details that are not important.

Read the story. Use the Reading Guide for tips. The tips will help you summarize and interpret figurative language as you read.

Reading Guide

What words does the writer use to describe the way the waves break on the shore?

What does Kerry see when she looks into the tidal pool? What words help you picture what she sees and how she feels?

How does the writer help you picture the minnows? What is this passage about? Summarize what happens in the passage.

AT THE BEACH

Kerry loved the beach. The beach was her friend. She felt so comfortable here. She loved to feel the wet sand squishing through her toes. She loved the smell of the air. She loved the way the waves patted the shore like a gentle hand.

What she loved most, though, was low tide. She would wait until the tide went out. Then she would lie on her stomach at the edge of a small **tidal** pool that the water left behind. She would gaze into the shallow water forever and ever.

Harmless little crabs scooted across the bottom of the pool. They were blurry clouds, stirring up dust in the sand. Tiny shrimp looked like pieces of glass. They zipped back and forth.

Minnows, or baby fish, swirled gracefully through the water like dancers at a **recital**. Silky ribbons of black, gray, and brown swished though the water. Sometimes they turned in slow circles. Sometimes they moved back and forth or side to side. Other times they spread out in a pattern. They were like a slow motion underwater fireworks show. Kerry couldn't take her eyes off them.

Answer the questions on the next page.

Practice the Skill 2

Practice interpreting figurative language by answering questions about the story you just read. Read each question. Circle the letter of the best answer.

1. When the writer says that the waves patted the shore like a gentle hand, the writer means the waves were —

   A flowing smoothly onto the sand

   B crashing loudly onto shore

   C rough and high

   D soft to touch

2. In the story, the words <u>forever and ever</u> mean —

   A for all time

   B for days and days

   C night and day

   D for a long while

3. The writer uses the image of blurry clouds to show you —

   A it was about to rain

   B how fast the crabs were moving

   C Kerry had dust in her eyes

   D Kerry was confused

4. Which two things are not compared in the story?

   A Sand and toes

   B Crabs and clouds

   C Shrimp and glass

   D Minnows and dancers

5. By comparing the swimming fish to fireworks, the writer means that the fish —

   A were making loud noises

   B were swimming away

   C were putting on a great show

   D were jumping out of the water

6. On a separate sheet of paper, explain what the figurative language in the last sentence of the story means.

LiON CUB aND PUPPY BECOME FriENDS

Koza the lion cub and Cairo the puppy like to play together.

SAN DIEGO, CA—Who says cats and dogs don't get along? A lion cub and puppy have become friends at the San Diego Wild Animal Park. They make quite an odd couple.

Koza is a lion cub. He needed a playmate. There were no other lions at the park. So, the park brought in a puppy named Cairo to play with him. Both animals were shy at first. Then the lion and puppy became good friends. "It probably took them about a week, more or less, to start playing," said park worker Autumn Nelson.

Cairo and Koza are like two peas in a pod. Sometimes they play for over four hours together. They love to run around and pounce on each other. Their favorite game is tug-of-war.

Write About It

Read this sentence from the article: *Cairo and Koza are like two peas in a pod*. This sentence has figurative language that compares two things. What does this sentence mean? Use clues from the article to write your answer.

Show What You Learned

Read this article about a special show. Then answer the questions on the next page.

A STOMPING GOOD TIME

The lights dim. The audience stops **chattering** like squirrels and quiets down. Soon, the theater is as dark as night. Then, a spotlight shines like the sun in the middle of the curtain.

A performer walks onstage and steps into the light. She leads the audience in clapping. At first, it's as simple as a game of paddy-cake. She claps. The audience claps. She claps again. The audience claps again. The game goes on and on. Everyone gets into it, even little kids.

The people in the audience are about to travel on a wild journey to an amazing world of noise. That's right! They have come for an evening of loud, crashing noise.

Have they lost their heads? Who would pay money to listen to noise? If you want a headache, stand in a school playground for fifteen minutes.

This isn't ordinary noise. This isn't an ordinary show. This is "STOMP."

In most plays, actors speak to tell a story. In musicals, actors sing and dance. "STOMP" uses music and dance to tell a story. The difference is that music doesn't come from instruments like a piano or a guitar. It doesn't come from the singing voices of the actors either. The performers in "STOMP" never say or sing a word. "STOMP" makes music from the noises that are all around us.

Everyday objects like trash can lids and hammers are instruments in the hands of the performers. The sounds are wild and loud. The sounds can also whisper when brooms are swished across the stage. All the sounds have a **rhythm** that moves the performers.

After a while, the audience doesn't hear noise. They hear only music. It is like the music of their everyday lives.

Read each question. Circle the letter of the best answer.

1. Why does the writer compare the audience to squirrels?

   A To show they are bored

   B To show they are scared

   C To show they are talking in a lively way

   D To show they are running around the theater

2. By comparing the spotlight to the sun, the writer helps you picture —

   A a bright yellow circle of light on the curtain

   B how hot it is in the theater

   C how large the stage is

   D how excited everyone is for the show to begin

3. Which phrase from the article means "is really enjoying"?

   A *is as dark as night*

   B *steps into the light*

   C *game goes on*

   D *gets into it*

4. The figurative language in this article suggests that the people in the audience —

   A are going on a long trip

   B are about to have a good time

   C do not know what the show is about

   D should get their money back

5. In the article, the writer compares going to see "STOMP" to —

   A getting a bad headache

   B losing your head

   C entering a world of noise

   D sitting in the dark

6. The phrase <u>Have they lost their heads</u> means —

   A they don't know what they're doing

   B they must be lost

   C they can't find their hats

   D they have forgotten who they are

7. In the story, the writer compares the sound of brooms swishing across the stage to a —

   A clap

   B piano

   C guitar

   D whisper

8. On a separate sheet of paper, explain what the last sentence of the article means.

Show What You Know

R3.3   Evaluate content by identifying whether events, actions, characters, and/or settings are realistic.

Before you begin this lesson, take this quiz to show what you know about real and make-believe. Read this passage about the writer Aesop. Then answer the questions.

AESOP AND HIS FABLES

Aesop lived in Greece over 2,500 years ago. He wrote hundreds of stories called fables. Most of his fables had animals as main characters. All of Aesop's fables ended with a moral, or lesson.

"The Fox and the Grapes" is about a thirsty fox. Fox sees some grapes growing above his head. He wants the juicy grapes, so he tries to jump up and grab them. He tries a couple times, then gives up. Before walking away, he says, "Those grapes are probably **sour,** anyway!"

In "The Lion and the Mouse," a mouse convinces a lion not to eat him. "Someday you might need my help," Mouse tells Lion. Later, Lion is captured by hunters and tied to a tree. Mouse chews through the ropes and frees Lion.

"The Ant and the Dove" is about a dove and an ant that help each other. First Dove saves Ant from drowning. She drops a leaf that Ant rides like a raft. Later, Ant saves Dove from a bird catcher.

Circle the letter of the best answer.

1. Which event really happened?

    A Mouse convinced Lion not to eat him.

    B Fox jumped up to get the grapes.

    C Ant rode a leaf like a raft.

    D Aesop wrote hundreds of fables.

2. Which event could not really happen?

    A A bird catcher tries to trap a dove.

    B A lion is captured by hunters.

    C A mouse convinces a lion not to eat him.

    D Aesop lived in Greece over 2,500 years ago.

3. Which character from the passage existed in real life?

    A Mouse

    B Aesop

    C Lion

    D Dove

4. Which of these is make-believe?

    A Fox says, "Those grapes are probably sour, anyway!"

    B Most of Aesop's stories had animals as main characters.

    C "The Fox and the Grapes" is about a thirsty fox.

    D All of Aesop's fables ended with a moral, or lesson.

LADDERS to SUCCESS

LESSON

8

Distinguishing Between Real and Make-Believe

Guided Instruction 1

R3.3   Evaluate content by identifying whether events, actions, characters, and/or settings are realistic.

Introduction

Something in a passage is **real** when it could happen in real life. Something in a passage is **make-believe** when it could not happen in real life. When you **distinguish between real and make-believe,** you tell what is real and what is make-believe.

To distinguish between real and make-believe,

- Look for details that describe the people, places, things, and events.
- Think about what could happen in real life and what could never happen.
- Decide what is real and what is make-believe.

Here's How

Read these sentences. What parts could be true? What parts could not happen in real life?

Jack was still very curious. He wanted to know what was at the top of the beanstalk, so he climbed it.

Think About It

1. I see that Jack is a curious boy. I see that Jack climbed the beanstalk.

2. I know that someone who wants to learn about something is curious. I know that a beanstalk is too small for a person to climb.

3. The detail that Jack was curious could be real. The detail that he climbed the beanstalk could not happen. That detail is make-believe.

Try This Strategy

Visualize

When you **visualize,** you form a picture in your mind.

- Think about how the writer describes people, places, things, and events.
- Use the details and descriptions to form pictures in your mind.

Read the story. Use the Reading Guide for tips. The tips will help you visualize and distinguish between real and make-believe as you read.

 Reading Guide

Think about the events. Real people might do these things.

Visualize Jack climbing the beanstalk. Picture a real boy trying to climb a real bean plant.

Think about whether giants or castles exist in real life.

Ask yourself whether this goose could lay golden eggs in real life.

JACK and the BEANSTALK

Jack's mom told him to sell their cow. On his way to the market, Jack met a man. The man asked Jack if he would trade the cow for seeds. The man said they were magical seeds.

Jack was a curious boy. He wanted to know if the seeds were magical, so he traded his cow. When Jack got home, he planted the seed. It sprouted right away. The seeds became a beanstalk. The beanstalk grew so tall that Jack couldn't see the top.

Jack was still very curious. He wanted to know what was at the top of the beanstalk, so he climbed it. Jack climbed high above the clouds. Finally, he got to the top. He saw a huge castle.

Jack was even more curious. He wanted to know what was in the castle, so he went in. Jack saw a giant and a goose that laid golden eggs. The man who gave Jack the beans was right. They *were* magic seeds.

Now use what you learned to distinguish between real and make-believe.

Answer the questions on the next page.

LADDERS to SUCCESS

LESSON

8

Distinguishing Between Real and Make-Believe

Practice the Skill 1

R3.3   Evaluate content by identifying whether events, actions, characters, and/or settings are realistic.

Practice distinguishing between real and make-believe with the story you just read.

EXAMPLE

Which could be true in real life?

A Jack traded his cow for seeds.

B Jack climbed a giant beanstalk.

C Jack planted magic seeds.

D Jack saw a magic goose.

Look for details about characters, settings, or events.

I read that Jack traded his cow for seeds. Then he planted the magic seeds and climbed a beanstalk.

Think about what could happen in real life. Think about what could never happen.

A boy could trade a cow for seeds. There is no such thing as magic seeds, a giant beanstalk, or a magical goose. A person couldn't climb a beanstalk.

Tell what is real.

The only detail that could be real is that Jack traded his cow for seeds.

Now read each question. Circle the letter of the best answer.

1. Which of these could happen in real life?

    A Jack climbed above the clouds.

    B The man gave Jack magic seeds.

    C Jack planted the seeds.

    D Jack saw a giant in the castle.

2. Which could never exist?

    A A beanstalk

    B A giant

    C A castle

    D A cow

3. Which of these could not happen?

    A The seeds became a beanstalk.

    B The seeds sprouted right away.

    C Jack met a man.

    D Jack traded his cow for beans.

4. Which of these could be real?

    A a giant that lives in a castle

    B a magic bean seed

    C a goose that lays golden eggs

    D a boy who trades a cow

They CAN Build It!

These sculptures of the Empire State Building and King Kong are made out of cans.

NEW YORK, NY—It takes a real "can-do" attitude to win this contest! It's the 13th Annual Design and Build Contest. At this contest, people use cans to make sculptures.

Cans can become anything from cars to castles. Someone made a sculpture of the **mythical** King Kong. The Empire State Building is an actual building in New York City. There's a model of that made out of cans, too.

How do these sculptures remain standing? Wood and plastic sheets help support them. Some cans are held in place with clear tape.

The cans are part of a food drive. People plan a sculpture. Then they buy the cans of food to make the sculpture with. When the event is over, the food goes to food pantries. The goal is to get people excited about helping others.

Write About It

Now practice the skill. Use information from this news article. Complete this graphic organizer by filling in what is real and what is make-believe.

Detail From Passage	Real or Make-Believe?
Empire State Building	
King Kong	
13th Annual Design and Build Contest	

LADDERS to SUCCESS

LESSON

8

Distinguishing Between Real and Make-Believe

Ladder to Success

R3.3   Evaluate content by identifying whether events, actions, characters, and/or settings are realistic.

Review

You have been learning the difference between **real and make-believe.** Some stories tell about things that could happen. These things are real. Stories can also tell about things that could never happen, like talking animals. These things are make-believe.

Review the steps you can use to distinguish between real and make-believe.

- Pay attention to the people, places, things, and events in a passage.
- If something could happen in real life, then it is real.
- If something could never happen in real life, then it is make-believe.

Practice 1

Read the following passage. As you read, think about the details. Then decide what is real and what is make-believe.

Dr. Seuss was a famous writer. Lots of kids have read his books. Many adults have read his books, too. Dr. Seuss wrote great books about silly things. In one book, a talking cat wears a tall hat and plays with some kids. The cat makes a big mess, but then he cleans it up.

Use the chart below to tell what could be real and what is make-believe.

Detail From Passage	Real or Make-Believe?
Dr. Seuss was a famous writer.	
Lots of kids have read his books.	
Lots of adults have read his books.	
Dr. Seuss wrote books about silly things.	
A talking cat plays with some kids.	
The cat makes a big mess.	
The cat cleans up the big mess.	

Practice 2

Read the story. Look for details that are real and details that are make-believe.

Gordo is my best friend. He used to be a robot. Gordo would help me with my chores. He could pick up one hundred toys at a time with his ten arms! One day, I couldn't find my slippers. I thought they were under my bed. I looked, but I couldn't see anything. It was too dark under there. Gordo picked my bed up with one of his arms. I found my slippers!

I always wished that Gordo could be a real boy and go to school with me. When I woke up one morning, my wish came true. Gordo wasn't a robot anymore. He had turned into a real boy!

Use this graphic organizer to distinguish between real and make-believe.

Details That Could Be Real	Details That Are Make-Believe

Practice 3

Read the story. Then distinguish between real and make-believe to answer the questions. Make a graphic organizer on a separate sheet of paper to organize your thoughts.

> "Tell me again, Dad!" said Timmy the Turtle. "Tell me about the time you beat Robbie's dad in a race."
>
> "Well," began Timmy's dad. "It was a long time ago. . ." Timmy's dad stopped and shifted in the chair. "Now, where was I? Ah, yes. It was a long time ago. . ."
>
> "Dad!" cried Timmy. "Hurry up! Tell the story!"
>
> "Oh, you're always in a rush," his dad said. "Slow and steady, that's what I say." Timmy's dad looked out the window and sighed. Then he turned back and began again. "OK. It was about thirty years ago, maybe longer. . ."
>
> "Dad, I get it. It was a long time ago. PLEASE get to the part about the race!" Timmy said.
>
> "Alright. I'm getting to it."
>
> Timmy moved closer. He loved this story. "Go ahead, Dad."
>
> "Ricky the Rabbit and I went to school together. We were about your age." Timmy's dad stopped and pointed. "Look at that sunset! I could stare at it for hours."
>
> "Please don't, Dad," said Timmy. "Tell me about the race."
>
> "OK," said Timmy's dad. "It was a long time ago. . ."

1. Explain how Timmy acts like a real boy. Explain how his father acts like a real man.

_____

_____

2. Describe the parts of this story that are make-believe.

_____

_____

3. Is this story real or make-believe? Tell why.

_____

_____

Guided Instruction 2

R3.3   Evaluate content by identifying whether events, actions, characters, and/or settings are realistic.

Things that are **real** can really happen. Things that are **make-believe** can never happen. When you read, you will come across details that are real. You will also come across details that are make-believe. Try to tell the difference between real and make-believe. You'll understand and enjoy the story better.

As you saw on pages 111–113, graphic organizers help you distinguish between real and make-believe.

- Think about the people, places, things, and events. Write them in the first column.
- Decide which things could be real. Write "real" beside them. Decide which things could not be real. Write "make-believe" beside them.

Read these sentences. Decide which details are real. Decide which details are make-believe.

Sometimes sailors got so sick that they would see things that weren't there. Some said they saw snakelike sea monsters.

Think About It

Detail	Real or Make-Believe?
sailors got sick	real
snakelike sea monsters	make-believe

Use Prior Knowledge

When you **use prior knowledge,** you use what you know to understand what you read.

- Think about the people, places, things, and events the author describes. Think of what you already know about them.
- Make connections between what you read and what you already know.

Read the story. Use the Reading Guide for tips. The tips will help you use prior knowledge and distinguish between real and make-believe as you read.

Reading Guide

Are these details real or make-believe?

What do you know about mermaids and unicorns? Are they real?

Do these explanations tell about real things or events?

What clues does the writer use to show that a detail is make-believe?

What Sailors Saw at Sea

Long ago, some sailors spent their entire lives on the ocean. They would sail back and forth across the ocean. It was very dangerous. Storms would wreck their ships. Pirates would steal their things. They also got sick very easily. Sometimes sailors got so sick that they would see things that weren't there. Some said they saw snakelike sea monsters. Others said they saw mermaids. Some talked about horned horses called unicorns.

Today we know that these creatures are not real. Some people think that the sailors saw real things, but not clearly. The sea monsters may have had the tentacles of a giant squid. The mermaids might have been sea cows, or manatees. Manatees may have looked like mermaids from far away. Some sailors just made up stories about what they saw. Viking sailors only pretended to see unicorns. They would sell fake unicorn horns to people all over Europe. The spiral horns were actually from a whale called a narwhal.

Answer the questions on the next page.

Practice the Skill 2

R3.3   Evaluate content by identifying whether events, actions, characters, and/or settings are realistic.

Practice distinguishing between real and make-believe by answering questions about the article you just read. Read each question. Circle the letter of the best answer.

1. Which is not true?

    A Sailors made up stories about what they saw.

    B Sailors saw mermaids.

    C Sailors saw real things, but not clearly.

    D Magical creatures don't exist.

2. Which happened in real life?

    A Pirates stole from sailors.

    B Sailors thought pirates were magical.

    C Sailors knew that sea mermaids were actually manatees.

    D Sailors captured and rode horned horses.

3. Which could be real?

    A Magical horned horses

    B Sea monsters

    C Giant squid

    D Mermaids

4. Which never happened?

    A Vikings sold actual unicorn horns.

    B Vikings tricked people into buying narwhal horns.

    C Sailors thought they saw magical sea creatures.

    D Sailors traveled across the ocean in ships.

5. Which is not real?

    A Sailors

    B Pirates

    C Narwhals

    D Mermaids

6. On a separate sheet of paper, write something that is real and something that is make-believe from the article.

NEWS FLASH!

Two-Headed Snake SOLD

This two-headed snake was sold for over $150,000.

ST. LOUIS, MO—Two heads really are better than one! A two-headed snake named "We" was sold at the World Aquarium in St. Louis. The snake sold for over $150,000. It had been with the aquarium for over six years. The money from the snake's sale will go toward education programs at the aquarium. The aquarium bought the snake for only $15,000.

Two-headed animals are rare, but they are real. Many of them have been found in the wild. Most do not live very long. This snake has lived for nearly seven years. Its two heads share the same stomach. Some believe that this has helped the snake live so long. The snake could live even longer. With the right care, the snake could live another ten years or more.

Write About It

This passage is about a two-headed snake. Are two-headed snakes real or make-believe? How do you know? Explain your answer on a separate sheet of paper.

Show What You Learned

Read the story about strange things that happen at Billy's house. Then answer the questions on the next page.

YOU CAN SAY THAT AGAIN!

"Dad, can I have five dollars?" I asked.

"Billy, you know that money doesn't grow on trees!" he answered.

When I looked out the window, I saw the strangest thing. In the corner behind our apartment building stood a maple tree. Where there used to be scraggly leaves, now there were bright green dollar bills! The branches used to be covered with prickly thorns. Now they were covered with shiny new quarters! I guess my dad was wrong.

The next day, I ran home from school. I was in a hurry to go check the tree. I forgot to close the front door. "Do you think you live in a barn?" Dad said.

All of a sudden, I heard a shocking sound from the living room. "Mooooo!" Another sound came from the kitchen. "Cluck. Cluck. Cluck!" It took us three hours to get rid of those animals!

I was glad the next day was Saturday. I needed a break. Dad came into my room to wake me up early, though. "Get up, lazy bones!" he said cheerfully. "Your closet isn't going to clean itself!"

"Uh-oh" I thought. As soon as the words came out of Dad's mouth, the closet doors popped open. Foamy bubbles poured out onto my bedroom floor. I guess my closet was going to clean itself.

What has been going on around here? I am going to have to be very careful about everything I do and say. For once, I don't think it would be funny if Dad said, "Don't stick your tongue out, or your face might freeze like that." No, I don't think I'd like that at all. From now on, I'm keeping my tongue in my mouth!

Read each question. Circle the letter of the best answer.

1. Which of the following could not be real?

   A A boy thinks he lives in a barn.

   B A boy is in a hurry to check a tree.

   C A maple tree stands behind the apartment.

   D A closet makes foamy soap bubbles.

2. Which of the following could happen?

   A The branches of the maple tree are covered with quarters.

   B Billy decides to keep his tongue in his mouth from now on.

   C The closet doors swing open on their own.

   D Chickens appear in the kitchen.

3. Which of these is make-believe?

   A A maple tree has scraggly leaves.

   B A boy runs home.

   C A closet cleans itself.

   D A father wakes up his son.

4. Which of the following could never be true?

   A The branches used to be covered with prickly thorns.

   B Billy heard a sound from the living room.

   C Dad woke Billy up cheerfully.

   D Billy's face froze when he stuck his tongue out.

5. Which of these events could not happen in real life?

   A A chicken suddenly appears out of thin air.

   B Billy looks out the apartment window.

   C Billy forgets to close the front door.

   D A cow makes a "Moo" sound.

6. Which sentence tells about something make-believe?

   A *It took us three hours to get rid of those animals!*

   B *Where there used to be scraggly leaves, now there were bright green dollar bills!*

   C *In the corner behind our apartment building stood a maple tree.*

   D *Dad came into my room to wake me up early, though.*

7. How do you know this story is make-believe?

   A Because the boy asks for money from his father

   B Because the father wants the boy to clean his room

   C Because magic things happen when someone repeats a silly phrase

   D Because animals make loud sounds

8. Pick one of the events in the story. On a separate sheet of paper, summarize the make-believe details.

Before you begin this lesson, take this quiz to show what you know about the author's purpose. First, read this passage about Kelly's morning. Then answer the questions.

A Quiet Morning

Kelly's alarm buzzed. She got up and dressed in the dark. The rest of the house was quiet. Everyone was asleep. Kelly poured herself a bowl of cereal. She sat at the kitchen table, eating quietly. A pink light was moving across the sky. Kelly ate quickly. Her aunt would be there to pick her up soon.

As Kelly was putting her bowl and spoon in the sink, she heard her aunt's car. She grabbed her coat and went to the front door. She opened it just as Aunt Beth was about to knock. Kelly put her finger to her lips. She knew they should leave quietly.

Kelly didn't talk during the ride. She just watched as day began. The soft pink glow she'd seen earlier had changed. Now it was a bright orange as the sun rose swiftly into the sky. They reached the river after about an hour of driving. The air was already warming. A **mist** was rising into the air.

Circle the letter of the best answer.

1. This passage is mostly about —

   A making breakfast

   B friendship

   C a long car ride

   D the start of a girl's day

2. Which detail is used to describe something?

   A A pink light was creeping across the sky.

   B Kelly ate quickly.

   C Her aunt would be there to pick her up soon.

   D She grabbed her coat.

3. The author's main purpose for writing is —

   A to tell a funny story about a girl and her aunt

   B to describe a girl's morning

   C to explain why the sun rises each day

   D to persuade you to get up to watch the sunrise

4. In the last paragraph, the author uses details to help you picture —

   A Kelly

   B her aunt

   C the river

   D the morning sky

Introduction

An author always has a reason for writing. This is the **author's purpose.** The author may write to **entertain,** so you enjoy what you read. The author might write to **persuade,** to make you believe something. Or the author might write to **inform,** or to tell you about something.

To determine author's purpose,

- Figure out what the passage or story is mostly about.

- Think about how the passage is written. Does it tell about funny or exciting events? Is it trying to get you to do or believe something? Does the author want you to learn something?

- Decide if the author's purpose is to entertain, persuade, or inform.

Here's How

Read these sentences. What is the author's purpose?

Sara told Dad that she was too big to play with dolls. That was bad news for Iggy. He lived in Sara's dollhouse, and it was headed for the attic!

Think About It

1. The passage tells about characters in a story.

2. The phrase "He lived in Sara's dollhouse" tells me this story has some things that are make-believe. The story is going to be fun.

3. The author's purpose is to entertain with a make-believe story.

Try This Strategy

Predict

You **predict** to guess what a passage will be about or what will happen.

- Read the title and first few sentences to see what the passage is about.

- Pause after reading each paragraph, and predict what might happen next. Check your predictions to see if you were correct.

Read the story. Use the Reading Guide for tips. The tips will help you predict and determine the author's purpose as you read.

Reading Guide

Read the title. Then read the first paragraph. Predict what the story will be about. Notice where the story takes place.

Pay attention to how Iggy moves around. Try to figure out what he'll do next.

Notice the word stinky. *Think about the way you feel when you read this word.*

Think about why the author wrote this story.

MOVING UP!

Sara told Dad that she was too big to play with dolls. That was bad news for Iggy. He lived in Sara's dollhouse, and it was headed for the attic!

Just before Dad grabbed the dollhouse, Iggy hopped out. First he rolled under the bed. After a few wiggles, he settled into a corner. It was too dark. Iggy looked around. Sara never wore her slippers any more. He scooted over and hopped inside one. Oh! Definitely NOT! Too stinky!

Iggy sighed. "If I could only stay in the dollhouse," he thought. Maybe the attic wouldn't be so bad after all. Iggy drifted up two flights of stairs. He climbed into the old dollhouse. Then he looked around. At first, all he saw was a bunch of old stuff. Then he noticed something amazing. Peeking out from all of the corners were dust balls just like him!

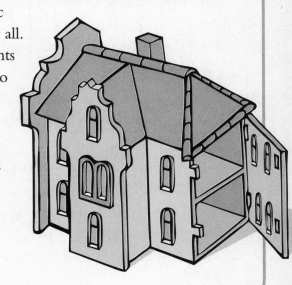

Now use what you learned to determine the author's purpose.

Answer the questions on the next page.

Practice the Skill 1

R3.3   Evaluate content by identifying the author's purpose.

Practice determining the author's purpose of the passage you just read.

EXAMPLE

What is the author's main purpose for writing this story?

A To explain how dust balls form

B To persuade readers to clean up their room

C To tell a fun story about a dust ball named Iggy

D To tell how people get rid of dust balls

What is the passage mostly about?

I see that most of the details tell about what Iggy does to find a new place to live.

How is the passage written? What kinds of words did the author use?

It seems like the writer wants to make me laugh. Iggy sounds cute.

Decide the author's purpose.

The purpose is to entertain readers with a fun story.

Now read each question. Circle the letter of the best answer.

1. The story is mostly about —

   A Sara's pet bunny

   B a girl who gets too old for her favorite toys

   C Iggy's search for a new place to live

   D a dollhouse that comes to life

2. Which word does the author use to make readers laugh?

   A *attic*

   B *settled*

   C *slippers*

   D *stinky*

3. What word is <u>not</u> a word the author uses to help you picture Iggy moving around?

   A *grabbed*

   B *hopped*

   C *wiggles*

   D *scooted*

4. Why does the author wait until the end of the story to tell what kind of character Iggy is?

   A To make readers feel sad

   B To surprise readers

   C To confuse readers

   D To trick readers

NEWS FLASH!

PIZZA BY PLANE

In Alaska, pizza is delivered by plane.

NOME, AK—"You buy, we fly!" That's the **slogan** for Airport Pizza. This pizza place is located in Nome, Alaska. It delivers its pies by plane.

This is great news for people who live hundreds of miles from Nome. Even hunters deep in the woods like to eat hot, fresh pizza.

H. Lee Griffin is the pilot of the plane. He says he's delivered many pizzas. There is one problem, though. The plane smells like pizza for a while after a delivery. That can attract bears!

Pizza by plane costs a little more than pizza from other places. The customers don't seem to mind, though. They love warm pies fresh from the oven. Airport Pizza is really taking off!

Write About It

Now practice the skill. Use information from this news article. Complete this graphic organizer to determine the author's purpose.

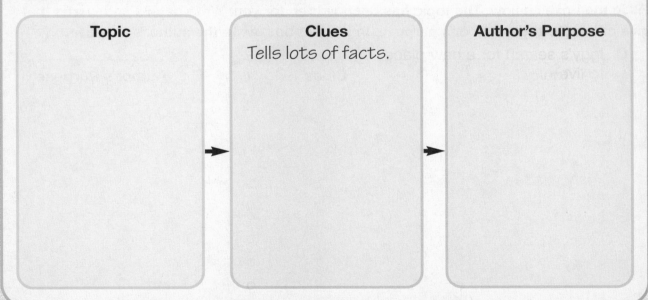

Topic	Clues	Author's Purpose
	Tells lots of facts.	

LADDERS to SUCCESS

LESSON

9

Determining
Author's Purpose

Ladder to Success

R3.3   Evaluate content by identifying the author's purpose.

Review

The author's purpose is the reason the author writes. When you **determine the author's purpose,** you figure out if the author wrote to entertain, to persuade, or to inform.

Review the steps you can use to determine the author's purpose.

- Think about the topic of the passage. Think about the main ideas.
- Think about how the passage is written. Is it funny or exciting? Does it make you feel a certain way? Does it tell you new information?
- Use these clues to tell the author's purpose.

Practice 1

Read the following passage. As you read, ask yourself, "Why did the author write this?" Is the author's purpose to entertain, to persuade, or to inform?

> Sit between a lamp and the wall. Turn your face until you make a shadow on the wall. Have a partner tape the paper where your shadow is. Then have your partner trace the outline of your profile. Don't move.
>
> Take the paper from the wall and tape it to a sheet of black paper. Carefully cut along the line, through both sheets. Glue the black paper to a background. Your silhouette is ready to frame!

Fill in the boxes below. The topic has been written for you. Write details and words that give clues about the author's purpose. In the last box, write the author's purpose.

Topic	Clues	Author's Purpose
silhouettes		

Practice 2

Read the passage. Think about how it is written. Pay attention to the kinds of words the authors chose to use.

Lots of things change when you go from place to place. People sound different. The food is different. Even the houses are different. Some houses are up on stilts. These houses are usually in places where there could be floods, such as near beaches and rivers. Some houses have flat roofs, and some houses have very steep roofs. Very steep roofs are usually seen in places where it snows a lot. A steep roof helps snow slide off. Otherwise, snow can get too heavy for the roof.

Use this graphic organizer to determine the author's purpose.

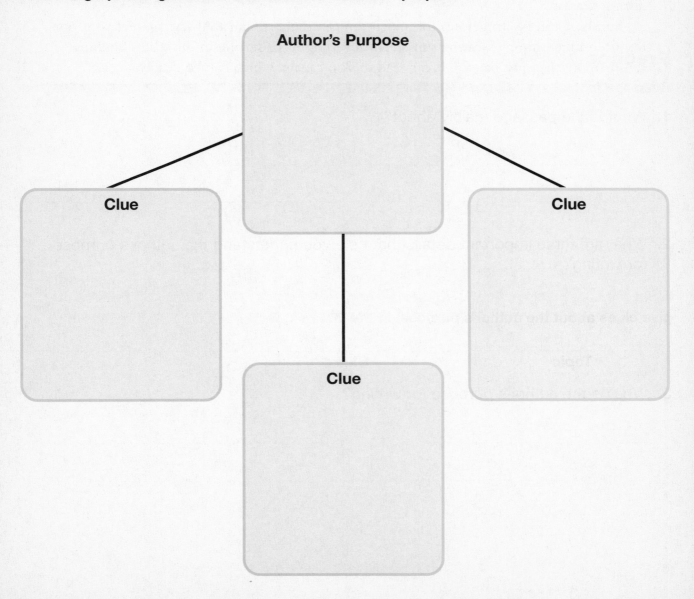

Practice 3

Read the passage. Then answer the questions to determine the author's purpose. Make a graphic organizer on a separate sheet of paper to organize your thoughts.

Sunshine is something that you need. It is also something that can cause you harm. You should always be sure to get enough sun. However, you should also follow a few simple rules to stay healthy.

Sunshine is important to your body in many ways. For example, sunlight helps your body make vitamin D. Vitamin D helps your body **absorb** calcium. Your body needs calcium for strong bones. Sunshine also helps keeps people happy. Studies show that people who don't get enough sunlight can become sad. Sunlight also tells your body when to sleep and when to wake up. Your body can tell day from night because there's sunlight during the day.

Sunshine can be dangerous. Too much sun can cause sunburn. Always protect your skin from too much sun by wearing sunscreen, covering up, or staying in the shade. Sunburn can be more than just painful. It can lead to skin cancer, which can be deadly.

1. What is the passage mainly about?

_____

_____

2. What are three important details that help you understand the author's purpose for writing?

_____

_____

3. What is the author's purpose for writing?

_____

_____

Guided Instruction 2

Introduction

An author writes to entertain, to persuade, or to inform. Thinking about the main idea of a passage, how it is written, and the words the author chose can help you **determine the author's purpose.**

As you saw on pages 125–127, graphic organizers can help you determine the author's purpose.

- Write what the passage is mostly about, or the main idea.
- Write words and phrases that give clues to the author's purpose.
- Write the author's purpose.

Here's How

Read these sentences. How do the words the author chose help you understand the author's purpose for writing?

Gloria McAllister's socks never matched. They were never the same color. They were never the same style. They were never even the same height. One day it would be one short pink one and one long purple flowered one.

Think About It

Main Idea	Clues	Author's Purpose
Gloria McAllister's socks never matched.	story told in a funny way one short pink one, one long purpled flowered one	to tell an entertaining story about a girl whose socks never matched

Try This Strategy

Summarize

When you **summarize,** you restate what you read in your own words.

- After you read each paragraph, state the main idea and details in your own words. If you need help, reread.
- After reading, summarize the important ideas of the passage.

Read the passage. Use the Reading Guide for tips that can help you summarize and determine the author's purpose as you read.

Reading Guide

What do you learn about Gloria at the beginning of the story?

What words describe how Gloria reacts to people's questions? How does this help you get to know Gloria better?

What happens at the end of the story? How does the ending make you feel?

Can you retell the most important parts of the story in your own words?

GLORIA MCALLISTER'S SOCKS

Gloria McAllister's socks never matched. They were never the same color. They were never the same style. They were never even the same height. One day it would be one short pink one and one long purple flowered one. Another day, she'd wear one blue sock from her soccer uniform and one furry orange slipper sock.

People often asked, "Why?"

Then she'd look at her feet and say, "Well, I'm sure I don't know!" She seemed to be just as surprised as everyone else.

It's said that when enough mistakes are made, something soon goes right. One day, Gloria's sock mismatches worked out just dandy.

It was the Fourth of July. Gloria was watching the town parade. Mr. Perriweather was standing next to her.

"Why, Miss McAllister," he exclaimed. "That's smart sock-wearing! How did you manage to wrap the American flag around your legs like that?"

Gloria looked down. Somehow, she'd managed to put on one sock from an old costume. It had white stars on a blue background. On her other foot was the sock for her softball uniform. That one had red and white stripes.

"Well, Mr. Perriweather," Gloria said, confused. "I'm sure I don't know!"

Answer the questions on the next page.

LADDERS to SUCCESS

LESSON

9

Determining Author's Purpose

Practice the Skill 2

R3.3   Evaluate content by identifying the author's purpose.

Practice determining the author's purpose by answering questions about the passage you just read. Read each question. Circle the letter of the best answer.

1. What is this passage mostly about?

   A Why it is important to wear matched socks if you want to be noticed

   B A girl named Gloria who enjoys dressing as a clown

   C Strange things that can happen when you wear the wrong socks

   D A girl named Gloria who has a strange habit of wearing the wrong socks

2. Which detail does the author use to help you get to know Gloria better?

   A *just as surprised*

   B *enough mistakes*

   C *just dandy*

   D *How did you manage*

3. What do you think the author wants you to know about Gloria?

   A She is embarrassed easily.

   B She's the best-dressed girl in town.

   C She's confused.

   D She's a show-off.

4. This passage does <u>not</u> have —

   A a funny main character

   B dialogue between characters

   C an important event

   D an author's opinion about a topic

5. What is the author's main purpose for writing?

   A To persuade readers to always wear matched socks

   B To entertain readers with a funny story

   C To describe funny looking socks

   D To inform readers with facts about socks

6. On a separate sheet of paper, choose two details from the passage and explain how they help you know the author's purpose.

Ringling Brothers Circus Makes Big Changes

The new Ringling Brothers show will tell a story.

TAMPA, FL—There is a new look at the circus these days. The Ringling Brothers and Barnum and Bailey Circus is making a change. The popular circus act is doing away with its three-ring format for the first time in its 136-year history. In addition, the show will be more than just a parade of elephants, clowns, and acrobats. Performers roaming the floor will work together to tell a story.

The circus made these changes so performers could connect with the audience. Ringling producer Kenneth Feld is happy about the changes. "For years we've been using the phrase 'an all new show,'" said Feld. "Now we can say we really mean it."

The new circus show cost $15 million to produce. It is the most expensive in Ringling's history. The circus plays to audiences of about 15,000 a night. They perform in 79 cities a year.

Write About It

Sometimes an author writes to give information. Sometimes an author writes to make the reader laugh or smile. Sometimes the author writes to convince you of something. Explain why the author wrote this article. Use a separate sheet of paper.

LADDERS to SUCCESS

LESSON
9
Determining
Author's Purpose

Show What You Learned

R3.3   Evaluate content by identifying the author's purpose.

Read this story about an elephant. Then answer the questions on the next page.

THE ELEPHANT'S CHILD'S NOSE

The Elephant's child was the most curious animal in the jungle. He bothered everyone in the family with his questions. One day he asked, "What does the crocodile eat for dinner?" Everyone got annoyed. "Stop asking questions!" they yelled meanly. So he wandered away, sad but very curious. Soon he met the Kolokolo bird. He asked him, "What does the crocodile eat for dinner?"

"Go to the banks of the grey-green Limpopo River and find the crocodile. Ask him yourself!" said the bird.

So the Elephant's child did. "What do you eat for dinner?" he asked the Crocodile.

"Come close so I can whisper in your ear," said the Crocodile.

The Elephant's child leaned in close. "You!" The Crocodile grabbed onto the Elephant's child's nose, which at the time was just a short stubby thing.

The Crocodile pulled. The Elephant's child pulled. The crocodile pulled harder. The Elephant's child pulled harder. They pulled and pulled all day. Finally, the Elephant's child was just too big and strong for the Crocodile. "Pop!" His nose popped out of the Crocodile's jaw. "Plop!" The Crocodile plopped back into the water. He floated away to find some dinner and some rest.

"Ow!" said the Elephant's child. His nose really hurt. And, my, how it was stretched! His little nose was now a five-foot trunk!

At first, the Elephant's child didn't like his new trunk. Then he realized that he could snatch up grass without bending or kneeling. He could swish flies off his back and ears. He could scoop up squishy mud onto his back to cool himself off. Proud of his new trunk, the Elephant's child headed back home.

When he got there, everyone was curious. "What happened?" They all asked. But the Elephant's child turned to them and yelled, "Stop asking questions!"

Read each question. Circle the letter of the best answer.

1. This story is mostly about —

   A an elephant with a sore nose

   B why the Elephant's child always asks everyone so many questions

   C what happens when the Elephant's child asks a question about Crocodile

   D how the Crocodile tricks the Elephant's child

2. From the details, you can tell that the author wants you to think that the Elephant's child is mostly —

   A curious

   B very sad

   C very proud

   D angry

3. How do you think the author wants you to feel about members of the Elephant's child's family?

   A They are funny.

   B They are not nice.

   C They ask too many questions.

   D They are helpful.

4. Which word from the story helped you to know the answer to question 3?

   A *meanly*

   B *helpfully*

   C *stubby*

   D *pesky*

5. The author probably wants you to read this story —

   A to form an opinion

   B to understand something

   C to learn facts

   D to enjoy yourself

6. One reason the author wrote the story might be to explain —

   A why children should not ask questions

   B why elephants have a long trunk

   C why crocodiles and elephants can't be friends

   D why crocodiles live in the river and elephants live on land

7. You can figure out the author's main purpose for writing because the story has —

   A opinions about elephants

   B details that describe real elephants

   C talking animals

   D tips for staying safe around crocodiles

8. On a separate sheet of paper, write the author's main purpose for writing.

Show What You Know

R3.2   Use knowledge of story structure, story elements, and key vocabulary to interpret stories.

Before you begin this lesson, take this quiz to show what you know about problems and solutions. First, read this story about two friends. Then answer the questions.

The Meaning of Friendship

Josh and Theo had to write a definition of *friendship* for homework. After 45 minutes, the only thing they had written was *Friendship is . . .*

For fun, they started wrestling on the floor. Then Josh's mom came in and snapped some pictures with her camera. The boys got embarrassed and went back to work.

"Maybe exercise will help," Theo said. "Let's shoot some hoops." Josh's mother followed them out with her camera. *Click. Click.* After an hour, the boys were tired.

"Let's get something to eat," Josh said. "Maybe that will help." Together, they made huge sandwiches. *Click. Click. Click.*

Food didn't solve their problem. Then Josh's mom brought the boys the pictures she had taken.

The next day, Josh and Theo turned in their definition.

At the top of their poster were the words *Friendship is . . .* Below were all the pictures Josh's mom had taken of them.

It was the perfect definition of friendship.

Circle the letter of the best answer.

1. What problem did Josh and Theo have in the first paragraph?

   A They didn't have enough time.

   B They had trouble doing their assignment.

   C They had too many good ideas.

   D They weren't getting along at all.

2. What is the first way the boys tried to solve their problem?

   A Eating sandwiches

   B Wrestling on the floor

   C Taking pictures

   D Playing basketball

3. What did Josh's Mom give the boys that helped them solve their problem?

   A Pictures

   B Sandwiches

   C Posters

   D Basketballs

4. What was their solution?

   A They looked up *friendship*.

   B They avoided their homework.

   C They used the pictures to show their friendship.

   D They wrote a poem.

Guided Instruction 1

Introduction

The characters in stories usually face problems. A **problem** is something that causes trouble. The **solution** is the way the character solves the problem.

To identify problems and solutions,

- Look for the trouble a character or person has.
- Look for the way the character or person tries to solve the problem. Does the solution have steps? Does the idea work?
- Did the character or person finally solve the problem? Tell how.

Here's How

Read these sentences. What problem does Pokie have? How does he solve it?

Once, Pokie was sitting on a log in the forest. Bear sat right down on top of him. Pokie wriggled his head out. "Excuse me!" he said.

Bear moved to the side. "Oops! Sorry, Pokie! Your brown fur blended in with the log."

Think About It

1. I see that Bear sat on Pokie.

2. Pokie said, "Excuse me!" to solve his problem.

3. Bear moved to the side. This solved Pokie's problem.

Try This Strategy

Predict

When you **predict,** you guess what will happen in a passage.

- Look at the title and read the first sentence. Try to predict what the passage will be about.
- While you read, think about your predictions. Were they correct? Change your predictions as you read.

Read the story. Use the Reading Guide for tips. The tips will help you predict and identify problem and solution as you read.

Reading Guide

How the Porcupine Got His Needles

Read the first paragraph. Find Pokie's main problem. Read the title again and predict how Pokie will solve his problem.

Read the dialogue carefully. The characters talk about each other's problems.

Think about the prediction you made when you started reading. Think about how Pokie solved his big problem. Compare the solution to your prediction.

Pokie was always being squished. No one looked out for him, and he was tired of it.

Once, Pokie was sitting on a log in the forest. Bear sat right down on top of him. Pokie wriggled his head out. "Excuse me!" he said.

Bear moved to the side. "Oops! Sorry, Pokie! Your brown fur blended in with the log."

Pokie rushed home and painted the ends of his fur white. "Now I won't blend in!" he said.

The next day, Pokie was walking through the garden. Raccoon tripped on a stick and plopped right onto him. Pokie squirmed halfway out. "Excuse me!"

Raccoon rolled off of Pokie. "Oops! Sorry Pokie! You were so soft I didn't know you were there."

Pokie rushed home. He opened his mending kit and made himself a prickly coat of needles. Then he went out for a stroll.

From then on, everyone was very careful not to squish Pokie!

Now use what you learned to identify problems and solutions.

Answer the questions on the next page.

Practice the Skill 1

R3.2   Use knowledge of story structure, story elements, and key vocabulary to interpret stories.

Practice identifying problems and solutions in the story you just read.

EXAMPLE

What is the first way Pokie tries to solve his problem?

A He makes a coat of needles.

B He sits on a log to think.

C He strolls through the forest.

D He paints the ends of his fur white.

Look for something difficult or something that goes wrong.

Pokie's problem is that people always bump into him.

Find what is done to try to solve the problem.

First, Pokie paints the ends of his fur white. He thinks this will make him stand out more.

Think about whether the solution solves the problem.

People keep on bumping into him. This solution does not solve the problem.

Now read each question. Circle the letter of the best answer.

1. How can you tell that painting Pokie's fur does not solve the problem?

   A Bear sat right down on top of him.

   B Pokie squirmed partway out.

   C Everyone was careful not to squish Pokie.

   D Raccoon falls on him.

2. What problem does Pokie have in the garden?

   A Raccoon falls on him.

   B He trips on a stick.

   C Bear sits on him.

   D He blends in with the log.

3. How does Pokie solve his problem?

   A He makes a coat of needles.

   B He paints his fur white.

   C He walks in the garden.

   D He rushes home to think about it.

4. What sentence tells you that Pokie's problem was solved?

   A *The next day, Pokie was walking through the garden.*

   B *From then on, everyone was very careful not to squish Pokie!*

   C *No one looked out for him, and he was tired of it.*

   D *Raccoon tripped on a stick and plopped right onto him.*

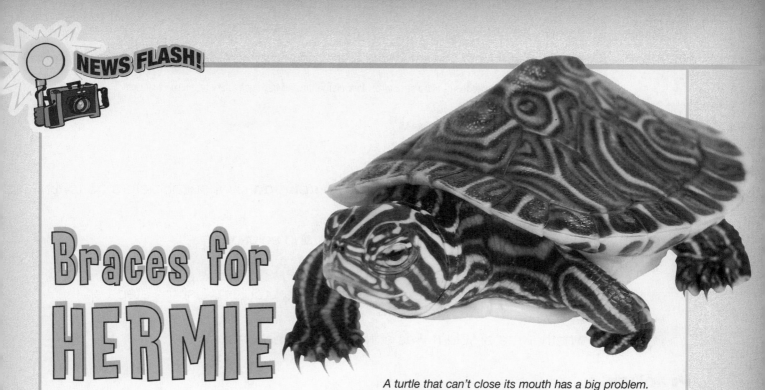

Braces for HERMIE

A turtle that can't close its mouth has a big problem.

WATERTOWN, NY—Hermie is a tiny turtle. He weighs about the same as a slice of bread. Hermie has done something very unusual. He got braces.

Hermie lives at the New York State Zoo. Zookeepers saw that Hermie's beak was not growing right. The tiny turtle couldn't close his mouth. Eating was becoming a big problem for him. Hermie's beak had to be fixed.

A vet and a dentist teamed up to help. They put pins and rubber bands in Hermie's mouth. This change should help Hermie's beak grow the right way.

Just like anyone else, Hermie will have to learn how to live with his new braces. Over time, zookeepers hope that the braces will help him eat better.

Write About It

Now practice the skill. Use information from this news article. Fill in the graphic organizer. Explain the problem Hermie had to solve.

Problem	Solution
	Hermie got braces.

Ladder to Success

R3.2   Use knowledge of story structure, story elements, and key vocabulary to interpret stories.

Review

A **problem** is something that causes trouble. The **solution** is what characters do to fix the problem or make it better.

Review the steps you can use to identify problems and solutions.

- As you read, look for the trouble someone faces.
- Look for the ways the characters try to solve the problem. List the steps or ideas they try.
- Decide whether the problem was solved. How was it solved?

Practice 1

Read the following passage. As you read, think about the problem that Jenna has. How does she solve the problem?

> Jenna's favorite jeans were ruined. That's what she got for wearing them while helping Dad work on the car. He'd warned her that she would get oil on them.
>
> Then she saw her mom was patching a hole in her brother's shirt. Jenna got an idea. She got her jeans. Jenna was thrilled when Mom said she could put a patch over the stain. Jenna thought it would look cool.

Think about the problem Jenna wants to solve. Write about it in the first box.

Problem	Solution
	Jenna's mom said she could put a patch over the stain.

Practice 2

Read the passage. What is the problem? How is the problem solved?

> "NO!" A gust of wind blew Jim's hat into the storm drain. Jim leaned over the curb. He looked into the drain. He shoved up his sleeve and poked his arm in. The hat was just beyond his fingertips.
>
> "What are you doing?" Lois asked. "Can I play?"
>
> "I'm not playing, Lois. My hat's in there."
>
> "Reach in and get it," Lois suggested.
>
> "I tried. My arm's too short." Jim looked at Lois. She was taller than he was. Maybe her arms were longer. "Will you try?"
>
> "Sure," Lois said. She knelt down and reached in. "Got it!" she called. She pulled Jim's hat out. "Now can we play?"

Fill in this graphic organizer to identify the solution.

Problem

Jim's hat falls into the drain and he can't reach it.

Solution

Practice 3

Read the passage. Then identify problems and solutions to answer the questions. Make a graphic organizer on a separate sheet of paper to organize your thoughts.

In 1888, a stray dog found its way into the Albany Post Office. The Post Office became his home, and the postal workers became his family. They named the dog Owney. He often rode mail wagons from the Post Office to the train station. Then he started riding the mail train back and forth to New York City. His friends were afraid he might get lost, so they gave him a collar and a tag. The tag said "Owney, Post Office, Albany, N.Y."

Owney made many new friends on his travels. They added tags to his collar to show where he had been. After a while, Owney's collar got too heavy. He could barely hold up his head. The Postmaster General made Owney a special vest. The tags could be attached all over the vest. That would spread out the weight.

As Owney traveled, he became famous. He traveled farther and farther. People loved him. They had parties and gave him awards. He visited China, Japan, Europe, and other places. Owney traveled more than 140,000 miles in his life!

1. What problem did the postal workers have when Owney started making longer trips back and forth to New York?

_____

_____

2. How did the postal workers solve that problem?

_____

_____

3. What problem did the Postmaster General solve? How did he solve it?

_____

_____

LESSON
10
Identifying Problems
and Solutions

Guided Instruction 2

R3.2   Use knowledge of story structure, story elements, and key vocabulary to interpret stories.

As you read stories and passages, you can identify **problems and solutions.** Pay attention to troubles or difficulties faced by characters or real people you read about. Think about how the problem is solved.

As you saw on pages 139–141, graphic organizers can help you identify problems and solutions.

- Describe the problem. Tell what is wrong or is causing trouble.
- Explain the steps taken to fix the problem. Tell if someone or something helped fix the problem.
- Tell whether the problem was solved.

Here's How

Read these sentences. What problem is solved?

The Maryland State House of today is the third one to stand in Annapolis. The first one burned down, so the governor had it rebuilt.

Think About It

Problem		Solution
The first Maryland State House burned down.		The governor had it rebuilt.

Try This Strategy

Monitor and Clarify

When you **monitor and clarify,** you check that you understand what you are reading.

- At the end of each paragraph, stop reading. Think about what you have learned. Do you understand all the information?
- If you do not understand what you have read, reread the paragraph.

Read the story. Use the Reading Guide for tips. The tips will help you monitor and clarify and identify problem and solution as you read.

 Reading Guide

A CLEVER DOME

Clarify what the first paragraph is about. What problems did the governor have?

The Maryland State House of today is the third one to stand in Annapolis. The first one burned down, so the governor had it rebuilt. By 1769, the second one was too small. The governor decided to have a new State House built.

The project began in 1772, but it was delayed. A few events slowed things down. First, there was a hurricane. Then, there was a war! Work got started again after the Revolutionary War ended, but things were still slow. The governor found someone to get the project back on track. His name was Joseph Clark.

Did Joseph Clark cause a problem or did he find a solution?

After the War, there was a shortage of metal. So Joseph Clark came up with a plan. He designed the dome to be made of wood. That wasn't too unusual back then. But there was also a shortage of nails.

Joseph had another clever idea. He built the dome so that the entire thing was held together with wooden pegs. The pegs were **reinforced** with iron strips. That dome stands today, with the original iron strips and wooden pegs. In this country, it is the largest wooden dome built entirely without nails!

Reread the writer's description of Joseph Clark's ideas. Were these good solutions?

Now use what you learned to identify problems and solutions.

Answer the questions on the next page.

Practice the Skill 2

R3.2   Use knowledge of story structure, story elements, and key vocabulary to interpret stories.

Practice identifying problems and solutions by answering questions about the article you just read. Read each question. Circle the letter of the best answer.

1. What problem did the governor face in 1769?

   A   The state house burned down.

   B   The state house was made of wood.

   C   The state house was too small.

   D   The state house collapsed.

2. How did the governor solve the problem?

   A   He decided to build a new one.

   B   He bought nails and wood.

   C   He designed a new dome.

   D   He started a war.

3. Which event first caused trouble for the new State House project?

   A   A fire

   B   A flood

   C   A war

   D   A hurricane

4. What second event slowed down the building of the State House?

   A   The Revolutionary War.

   B   A large fire

   C   The Civil War

   D   A wood shortage

5. How did the governor solve his problem?

   A   He designed a dome made of solid wood.

   B   He decided that the new State House was too small.

   C   He hired Joseph Clark to get things back on track.

   D   He held a contest to design a new State House.

6. On a separate sheet of paper, describe the main problem Joseph Clark faced when building the dome. Explain two things he did to solve that problem.

50,000 CROWS

Thousands of crows come to roost in Lancaster County each year.

LANCASTER COUNTY, PA—Some residents in Lancaster County have **relocated.** Lancaster County in Pennsylvania was successful in sending over 50,000 crows away from its busy downtown areas. The **pesky** crow population has been reduced to a reasonable number of 10,000 crows.

Wildlife officials found several ways to bring the population under control. Officials had some success hanging dead crows from trees to scare other crows away. Officials also used flashes of fire and recordings of crow distress calls to scare away large flocks.

But not all methods were successful. When wildlife officials tried using poison to lower the crow population, it didn't work. Instead, it angered some local residents.

Residents are enjoying the peace and quiet now. It may be short-lived, however. The crows are expected to return in full force next year.

Write About It

Lancaster County had a big problem. It had too many crows! On a separate sheet of paper, write three solutions officials used to solve the problem.

LADDERS to SUCCESS

LESSON
10
Identifying Problems and Solutions

Show What You Learned

R3.2   Use knowledge of story structure, story elements, and key vocabulary to interpret stories.

Read this story about a mystery. Then answer the questions on the next page.

THE NEWSPAPER MYSTERY

Ralph Simpson was upset. He hadn't received a single issue of his newspaper. He called the newspaper office. They said his paper was being sent.

At first, Ralph thought the paperboy had bad aim. Ralph checked the bushes and under the front porch. He even checked the roof. No papers. Maybe someone was stealing the newspapers from Ralph's yard.

On Monday, Ralph got up early. Hidden behind the window curtain, he watched and waited. Right on time, the paperboy came by and tossed the folded paper. It landed with a thud on the porch, right in front of Ralph's front door. Aim wasn't the problem. It had to be a thief.

Ralph kept watching, but no one came to snatch his paper. He went upstairs for his robe. Tying the sash, he opened the door to get the paper. It was gone! Ralph was furious!

On Tuesday, Ralph waited again. This time, he had his robe on. As soon as the paper thudded onto the porch, Ralph walked to the front hall. As he unlocked the door, he heard a rustling on the porch. He yanked open the door.

But he wasn't fast enough.

Ralph had had enough! On Wednesday, he put on his robe and brought a chair out to the porch. At 6:00 AM, the paperboy tossed the paper. Ralph never took his eyes off the paper. Just as he began to wonder if he was crazy, a squirrel ran up the porch steps, grabbed the paper, and ran back down the steps. Ralph chased the squirrel to an oak tree in the backyard. About halfway up the tree, he saw a hole in the trunk. In that hollow space, Ralph could see headlines from the past three weeks!

Read each question. Circle the letter of the best answer.

1. What is the main problem in this story?

    A   Ralph's paperboy is always late.

    B   Ralph doesn't like squirrels.

    C   Ralph isn't getting his newspaper.

    D   Ralph can't find his bathrobe.

2. What is the first thing Ralph does to try to solve his problem?

    A   He calls the newspaper.

    B   He chases a squirrel.

    C   He puts on his bathrobe.

    D   He looks in a tree.

3. How does Ralph check if the problem is bad aim?

    A   He calls the newspaper and asks if they know.

    B   He looks in the bushes, under the porch, and on the roof.

    C   He opens the door quickly so he can see the boy's face.

    D   He brings a chair onto his front porch and waits.

4. What problem does Ralph have on Monday?

    A   The paperboy never comes by to deliver the paper.

    B   The newspaper ends up under the front porch.

    C   By the time he puts on his robe, the paper is gone.

    D   He can't see from behind the window curtains.

5. What does Ralph do differently on Tuesday?

    A   He leaves the door unlocked.

    B   He sits outside.

    C   He checks the roof.

    D   He puts his robe on first.

6. What problem does Ralph have on Tuesday?

    A   He forgets to put on his bathrobe.

    B   He doesn't open the door fast enough.

    C   The door is stuck.

    D   The paperboy is late.

7. Why does Ralph put on his robe and sit on the porch on Wednesday?

    A   He doesn't want to miss the thief.

    B   He is tired of sitting in the house.

    C   He can't get a good enough view.

    D   He wants to question the paperboy.

8. On a separate sheet of paper, list the steps Ralph takes to solve his problem.

Glossary

absorb to soak up or take in (Lesson 9)

author's purpose the reason that an author writes a story or passage (Lesson 9)

cause and effect A cause is an event that makes something happen. The effect is what happens. (Lesson 3)

champion a person who wins a contest (Lesson 1)

chatter to talk about unimportant things (Lesson 7)

clump a group of things close together (Lesson 2)

collapse to fall down because of being weak (Lesson 2)

commotion a noisy and confused situation (Lesson 2)

compare and contrast to find ways things are alike and different (Lesson 1)

compute to find an answer using math (Lesson 1)

context clues words that help you figure out the meaning of words that you don't know (Lesson 4)

convince to say things to make someone do something (Lesson 3)

crow's nest a platform high up on a ship or boat from which a person can see very far (Lesson 7)

culprit a person who has done something wrong (Lesson 3)

diabetes a health problem that causes there to be too much sugar in the blood (Lesson 2)

draw conclusions an idea you figure out from details you read (Lesson 6)

entertain to say something that is fun and enjoyable (Lesson 9)

expert a person who is knowledgeable about something (Lesson 3)

feat an act that requires great skill and courage (Lesson 1)

fiber a small material that is part of cloth and string (Lesson 3)

figurative language words that create an image in a reader's head (Lesson 7)

gather to bring together in one place (Lesson 1)

imitate to be or look like someone else (Lesson 5)

inform to tell someone facts about something (Lesson 9)

larva a newly hatched insect that hasn't yet grown wings (Lesson 2)

main idea and details the most important idea or event of a passage or paragraph and the facts or events that support it (Lesson 5)

mist a fog (Lesson 9)

molasses a dark, sticky syrup made from sugar (Lesson 3)

monitor and clarify to make sure that you understand what you are reading (Lesson 3, Lesson 5, Lesson 6, Lesson 10)

mural a large painting on a wall (Lesson 5)

mysterious having a secret that cannot be explained (Lesson 6)

mythical imaginary or make-believe
(Lesson 8)

nutrient a material that a plant or animal can use to live or grow (Lesson 5)

official having been said by someone who is an expert or authority on something (Lesson 2)

permanent lasting for a long time without changing (Lesson 5)

permission the act of saying it is alright for someone to do something (Lesson 6)

persuade to say something to lead someone to agree with an opinion (Lesson 9)

pesky annoying and troublesome
(Lesson 10)

predict to think about what you have read and what might happen next (Lesson 5, Lesson 9, Lesson 10)

problems and solutions A problem is something that causes trouble. A solution is how the problem is solved. (Lesson 10)

process to calculate based on incoming information (Lesson 1)

pupa an insect inside a cocoon that is changing into an adult (Lesson 2)

raptor a bird that kills animals for food
(Lesson 2)

real and make-believe the things in a passage that could happen in real life and the things that could never happen in real life (Lesson 8)

recital a performance of music or dance (Lesson 7)

regenerate to grow back again after being lost (Lesson 2)

reinforce to strengthen and support
(Lesson 10)

relocate to move to a different place and stay there for a long time (Lesson 10)

reservoir a lake that is used to store water for drinking and other purposes
(Lesson 3)

routine the things someone usually does (Lesson 5)

rhythm a pattern of sounds in music
(Lesson 7)

scan and skim to look through a passage quickly to get an idea of what it is about (Lesson 1, Lesson 4)

schedule to plan to do something at a specific time (Lesson 1)

sequence the order in which things happen (Lesson 2)

shimmer to give off a soft and changing light (Lesson 7)

slogan a short phrase that explains the goals of a person or group (Lesson 9)

sour having a sharp taste that is not sweet (Lesson 8)

summarize to retell the most important parts of a story or passage in your own words (Lesson 2, Lesson 7, Lesson 9)

temporary lasting for only a short time
(Lesson 5)

tidal having to do with waves from the ocean that happen at the same time every day (Lesson 7)

translate to understand the meaning of words and say what they mean using a different language (Lesson 2)

use prior knowledge to use what you know to understand what you read (Lesson 1, Lesson 4, Lesson 6, Lesson 8)

utensil a tool that is used in a kitchen, especially one used for eating (Lesson 5)

vapor air that is wet (Lesson 3)

visualize to picture in your mind what you are reading (Lesson 2, Lesson 3, Lesson 7, Lesson 8)

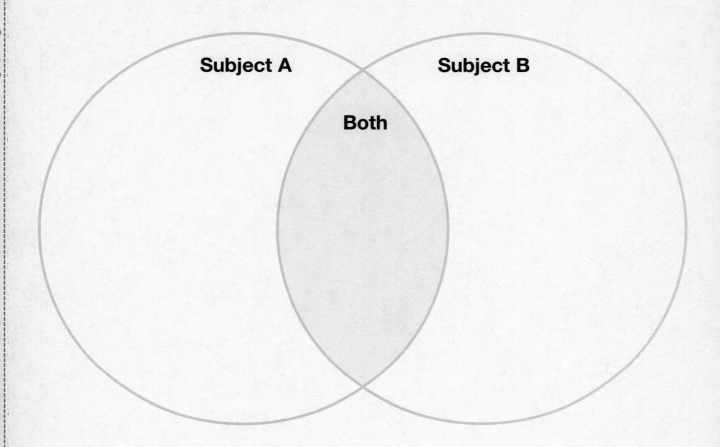

Subject A

Subject B

Both

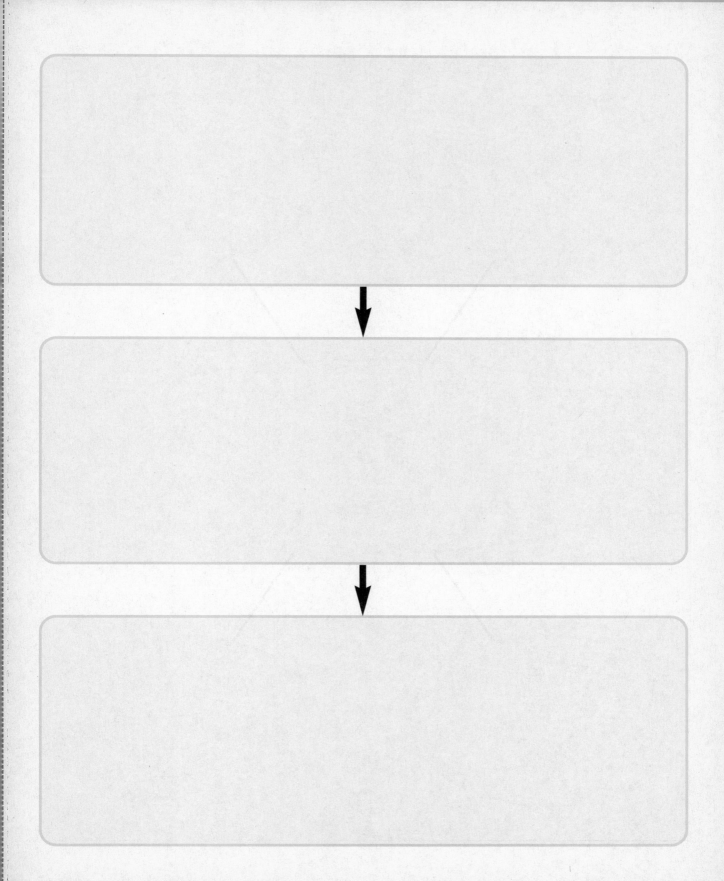

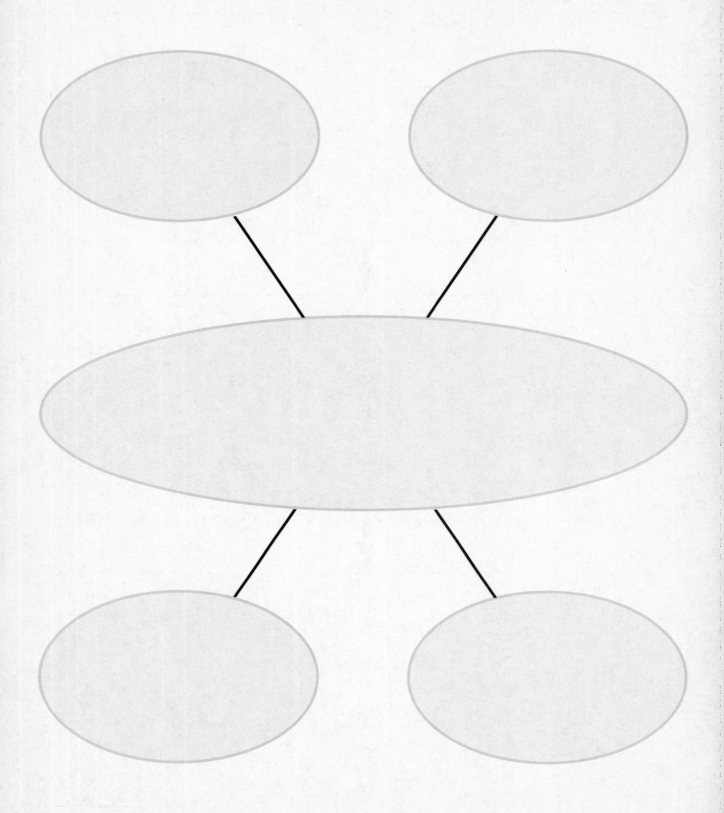

1.

2.

3.

4.

5.

6.

7.

8.

9.

10.

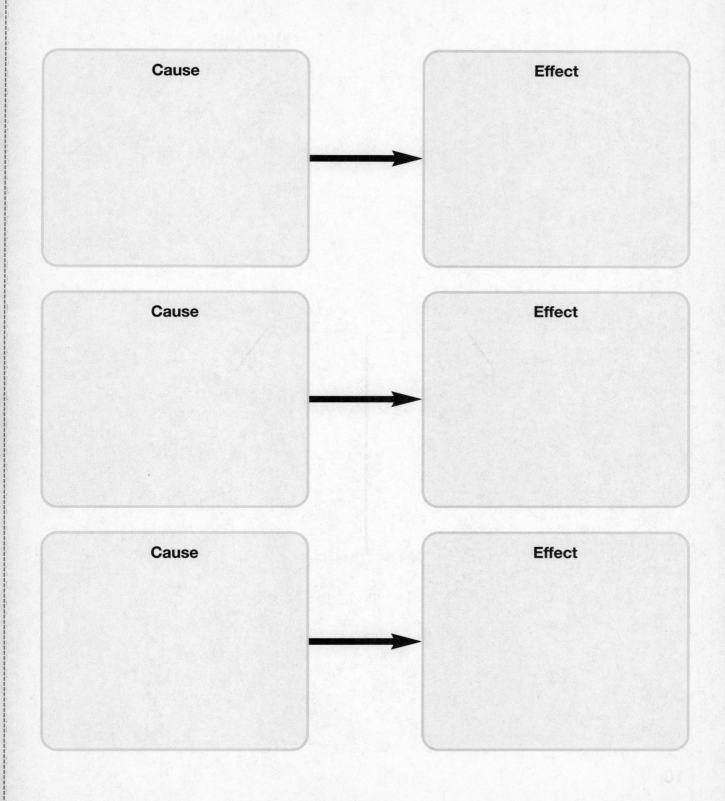

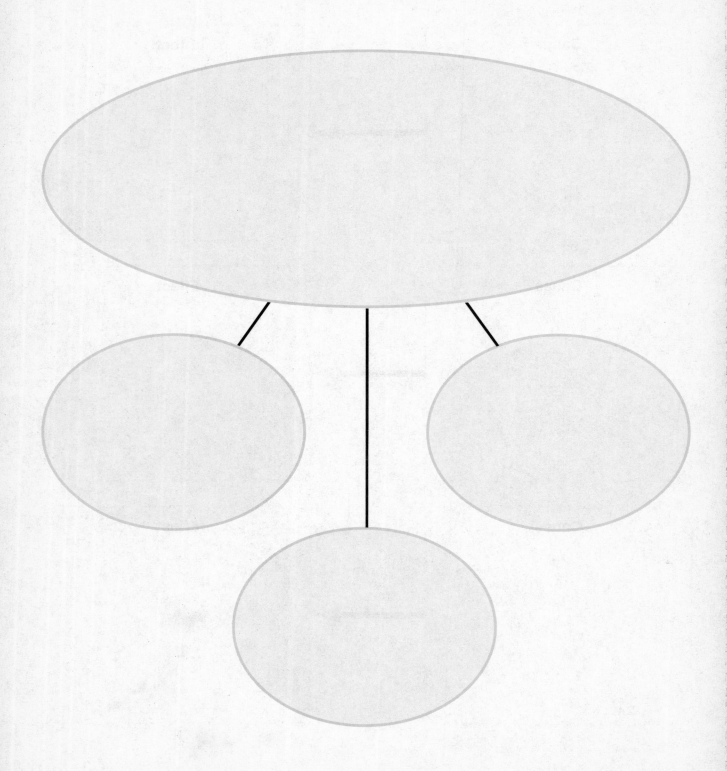